INTERNATIONAL TRAVEL AND HEALTH

INTERNATIONAL TRAVEL AND HEALTH

Vaccination Requirements and Health Advice

Situation as on 1 January 1995

WORLD HEALTH ORGANIZATION
GENEVA
1995

The information given in this publication is valid on the date of issue. It should be kept up to date with the notes of amendments published in the Weekly Epidemiological Record.

Any comments or questions concerning this publication should be addressed to:

Epidemiological Surveillance
and Statistical Services
World Health Organization
1211 Geneva 27, Switzerland

WHO Library Cataloguing in Publication Data

International travel and health : vaccination requirements and health advice : situation as on 1 January 1995.

1. Communicable disease control   2. Travel   3. Vaccination

ISBN 92 4 158020 8   (NLM Classification: WA 110)
ISSN 0254-296X

PRINTED IN SWITZERLAND
94/10204 – Atar – 12 000
94/10204 – Atar – 5500

CONTENTS

1. PREFACE

In recent years there has been a tremendous increase in the number of people travelling between the various countries of the world, and, in view of this, it is particularly important that health authorities are kept up to date on the changing immunization requirements and other prophylactic measures for travellers intending to go abroad.

There has been an increase not only in the volume but also in the speed of travel; thus with modern air transport, travellers infected in one country may still feel quite well when they arrive in another, if they are still only in the early stages of an illness. In these circumstances, the surveillance and other precautions taken at ports of arrival are often ineffective. Nowadays, also, tourists are able to penetrate areas of the world that were previously infrequently visited and these places may present hazards for which the inexperienced tourist is ill prepared.

This booklet is addressed to national health administrations that have the responsibility for providing advice on the health hazards of international travel, and to the practising physicians, travel agencies, shipping companies, airline operators, and other bodies who are called upon to give advice in individual cases. In addition to summarizing the vaccination requirements of individual countries, the booklet covers certain health hazards to which the traveller may be exposed and indicates the areas in which these hazards are most likely to occur. This is particularly important with malaria, which has continued to cause serious problems in recent years. It also recommends precautions that the wise traveller should take when visiting unfamiliar places.

This booklet focuses essentially on prevention. To a lesser extent, the epidemiological information it contains may also be used for diagnostic purposes.

2. VACCINATION REQUIREMENTS

2.1 International Health Regulations

The International Health Regulations adopted by the Twenty-second World Health Assembly in 1969 represent a revised and consolidated version of the previous International Sanitary Regulations.[1]

The purpose of the International Health Regulations is to help prevent the international spread of diseases and, in the context of international travel, to do so with the minimum of inconvenience to the passenger. This requires international collaboration in the detection and reduction or elimination of the sources from which infection spreads rather than attempts to prevent the introduction of disease by legalistic barriers that over the years have proved to be ineffective. Ultimately, however, the risk of an infective agent becoming established in a country is determined by the quality of the national epidemiological services and, in particular, by the day-to-day national health and disease surveillance activities and the ability to implement prompt and effective control measures.

No regulations can be expected to foresee every disease eventuality and, in certain situations, diseases and conditions other than those covered by the International Health Regulations may be of concern to national health authorities and the travelling public. The International Health Regulations obviously cannot refer specifically to diseases that were not known at the time they were last revised; this is the case with acquired immunodeficiency syndrome (AIDS). Nevertheless, any requirement for an HIV antibody test certificate ("AIDS-free certificate") is contrary to the Regulations, since Article 81 states that "no health document, other than those provided for in these Regulations, shall be required in international traffic".

It is hoped that the information provided in this booklet will enable health administrations to determine, on epidemiological grounds, the actions that should be taken and to advise travellers accordingly.

---

[1] *International Health Regulations (1969): Third annotated edition.* Geneva, World Health Organization, 1983, 79 pp.

2.2 Smallpox

> The eradication of smallpox was confirmed by WHO more than 10 years ago. Smallpox vaccination is *no longer indicated,* and may be dangerous to those who are vaccinated and those in close contact with them.

2.3 Cholera

> Vaccination against cholera cannot prevent the introduction of the infection into a country. The World Health Assembly therefore amended the International Health Regulations in 1973 so that *cholera vaccination should no longer be required of any traveller.*

The International Certificate of Vaccination no longer provides a specific space for indication of cholera vaccination. The protection conferred by currently available parenteral cholera vaccines is incomplete, unreliable and of short duration, and their use is therefore not recommended. Two oral cholera vaccines have recently become commercially available in a few countries. As trials of these vaccines are continuing, WHO has not yet formulated recommendations on their use. Vaccination is therefore not recommended as a means of personal protection against cholera. Moreover, there is no evidence that currently available vaccines decrease the quantity of *Vibrio cholerae* excreted by people with asymptomatic infection or chronic carriers.

2.4 Yellow fever vaccination certificate[1]

Urban and jungle yellow fever occur only in parts of Africa and South America (see maps 1 and 2, pp. 14 and 15). Urban yellow fever is an epidemic viral disease of humans transmitted from infected to susceptible persons by the *Aedes aegypti* mosquito. Jungle yellow fever is an enzootic viral disease transmitted among nonhuman primate hosts, and occasionally to humans, by a variety of mosquito vectors.

A yellow fever vaccination certificate is now the only certificate that should be required in international travel, and then only for a limited number of travellers.

Many countries require a valid International Certificate of Vaccination from travellers arriving from infected areas or from countries with infected areas, or who have been in transit through those areas. Some countries require a certificate from all entering travellers, including those in transit.

---

[1] See also section 5.4, "Sexually transmitted infections, including HIV (AIDS)", pp. 64–67.

Although there is no epidemiological justification for this latter requirement, which is clearly in excess of the International Health Regulations, travellers may find that it is strictly enforced, particularly for people arriving in Asia from Africa or South America.

On the other hand, *vaccination is strongly recommended for travel outside the urban areas of countries in the yellow fever endemic zone (maps 1 and 2, pp. 14 and 15), even if these countries have not officially reported the disease and do not require evidence of vaccination on entry.* Practitioners should note that the actual areas of yellow fever virus activity far exceed the infected zones officially reported and that, in recent years, fatal cases of yellow fever have occurred in unvaccinated tourists visiting rural areas within the yellow fever endemic zone.

The vaccination has almost total efficacy, while the case fatality rate for the disease is more than 60% in adults who are not immune. Tolerance of the present vaccine is excellent. The only contraindication to its use, apart from true allergy to egg protein, is cellular immunodeficiency (congenital or acquired, the latter sometimes being only temporary).

The vaccination certificate is valid only if it conforms with the model reproduced on pp. 12–13, and if the vaccine has been approved by WHO and administered at an approved Yellow Fever Vaccinating Centre.[1]

The period of validity of an international certificate of vaccination against yellow fever is 10 years, beginning 10 days after vaccination. If a person is revaccinated before the end of this period, the validity is extended for a further 10 years from the date of revaccination. If the revaccination is recorded on a new certificate, travellers are advised to retain the old certificate for 10 days until the new certificate becomes valid.

---

[1] *Yellow-fever vaccinating centres for international travel. Situation as on 1 January 1991.* Geneva, World Health Organization, 1991.

MODEL OF AN INTERNATIONAL CERTIFICATE OF VACCINATION OR REVACCINATION AGAINST YELLOW FEVER

The certificate must be *printed* in English and French; an additional language may be added. It must be *completed* in English or French; an additional language may be used.

The international certificate of vaccination is an *individual* certificate. It should not be used collectively. Separate certificates should be issued for children; the information should not be incorporated in the mother's certificate.

An international certificate is valid only if the yellow-fever vaccine used has been approved by WHO and if the vaccinating centre has been designated by the national health administration for the area in which the centre is situated and so recorded with WHO. (See the 1991 WHO publication *Yellow-fever vaccinating centres for international travel*.) The date should be recorded in the following sequence: day, month, year, with the month written in letters, e.g., 8 January 1991.

A certificate issued to a child who is unable to write should be signed by a parent or guardian. For illiterates, the signature should be indicated by their mark certified by another person.

Although a nurse may carry out the vaccination under the direct supervision of a qualified medical practitioner, the certificate must be signed by the person authorized by the national health administration. The official stamp of the centre is not an accepted substitute for a personal signature.

> *Signature of person vaccinated*
> *Signature de la personne vaccinée*

> *e.g.: 8 January 1991*
> *ex.: 8 janvier 1991*

> *Signature required*
> *(rubber stamp not accepted)*
> *Signature exigée (le cachet*
> *n'est pas suffisant)*

> *Official stamp*
> *Cachet officiel*

WHO 881091

INTERNATIONAL CERTIFICATE OF VACCINATION OR REVACCINATION AGAINST YELLOW FEVER

CERTIFICAT INTERNATIONAL DE VACCINATION OU DE REVACCINATION CONTRE LA FIÈVRE JAUNE

his is to certify that / e soussigné(e) certifie que   Ole OLSEN

hose signature follows / ont la signature suit   *O. Olsen*

date of birth / né(e) le   8 Nov. 1945   sex / sexe   M

as on the date indicated been vaccinated or revaccinated against yellow fever.
été vacciné(e) ou revacciné(e) contre la fièvre jaune à la date indiquée.

Date	Signature and professional status of vaccinator / Signature et titre du vaccinateur	Manufacturer and batch no. of vaccine / Fabricant du vaccin et numéro du lot	Official stamp of vaccinating centre / Cachet officiel du centre de vaccination
8 January 1991	Dr John Doe M.D.	R.I.V. 63007	*[official stamp]*
2			
3			

This certificate is valid only if the vaccine used has been approved by the World Health Organization and if the vaccinating centre has been esignated by the health administration for the territory in which that centre is situated.

The validity of this certificate shall extend for a period of ten years, beginning ten days after the date of vaccination or, in the event of a vaccination within such period of ten years, from the date of that revaccination.

This certificate must be signed in his own hand by a medical practitioner or other person authorized by the national health administration ; his ficial stamp is not an accepted substitute for his signature.

Any amendment of this certificate, or erasure, or failure to complete any part of it, may render it invalid.

Ce certificat n'est valable que si le vaccin employé a été approuvé par l'Organisation mondiale de la Santé et si le centre de vaccination a été abilité par l'administration sanitaire du territoire dans lequel ce centre est situé.

La validité de ce certificat couvre une période de dix ans commençant dix jours après la date de la vaccination ou, dans le cas d'une vaccination au cours de cette période de dix ans, le jour de cette revaccination.

Ce certificat doit être signé de sa propre main par un médecin ou une autre personne habilitée par l'administration sanitaire nationale, un cachet ficiel ne pouvant être considéré comme tenant lieu de signature.

Toute correction ou rature sur le certificat ou l'omission d'une quelconque des mentions qu'il comporte peut affecter sa validité.

MAP 1. YELLOW FEVER ENDEMIC ZONE IN AFRICA

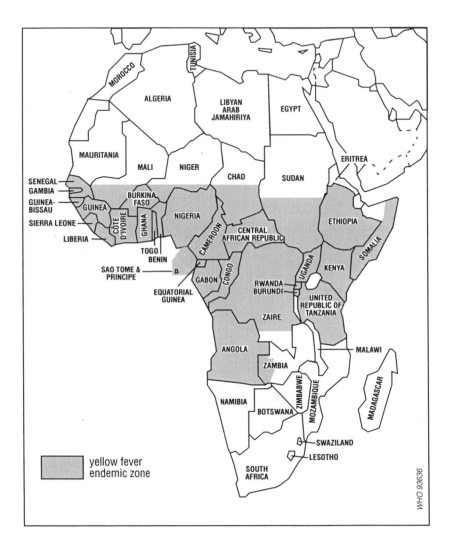

yellow fever endemic zone

WHO 93636

MAP 2. YELLOW FEVER ENDEMIC ZONE
IN THE AMERICAS

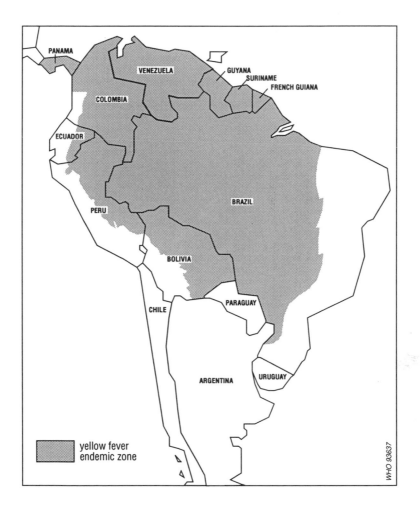

NOTE: The "yellow fever endemic zones" are areas where there is a potential risk of infection on account of the presence of vectors and animal reservoirs. Some countries consider these zones as "infected" areas, and require an international certificate of vaccination against yellow fever from travellers arriving from these areas. Maps 1 and 2 have therefore been included for this practical reason. See also section 2.4, "Yellow fever vaccination certificate", pp. 10–11.

3. COUNTRY LIST OF VACCINATION CERTIFICATE REQUIREMENTS AND INFORMATION ON THE MALARIA SITUATION

Smallpox

No country any longer requires a certificate of vaccination against smallpox.

Cholera

No country or territory any longer requires a certificate of vaccination against cholera.

Yellow fever

A certificate of vaccination against yellow fever is the only certificate that should be required for international travel. The requirements of some countries are in excess of the International Health Regulations. However, vaccination against yellow fever is strongly recommended to all travellers who intend to go to places other than the major cities in the countries where the disease occurs in man or is assumed to be present in primates (see pp. 10–11 and maps 1 and 2, pp. 14–15).

Malaria

Epidemiological details are given for all countries with malarious areas (geographical and seasonal distribution, altitude, predominant species, status of resistance). The recommended chemoprophylactic regimen is also indicated. The following abbreviations are used: – = no chemoprophylaxis necessary; CHL = chloroquine; C+P = chloroquine plus proguanil; MEF = mefloquine; DOX = doxycycline. Important advice on protective measures is given on pp. 67–82, and especially on pp. 71–73.

AFGHANISTAN

Yellow fever – A yellow fever vaccination certificate is required from travellers coming from infected areas.

Malaria – Malaria risk–predominantly in the benign *(Plasmodium vivax)* form–exists from May through November below 2000 m. Chloroquine-resistant *P. falciparum* reported.
   Recommended prophylaxis: C+P.

ALBANIA

Yellow fever – A yellow fever vaccination certificate is required from travellers over 1 year of age coming from infected areas.

ALGERIA

Yellow fever – A yellow fever vaccination certificate is required from travellers over 1 year of age coming from infected areas.

Malaria – Malaria risk is limited. Two small foci *(P. vivax)* have been reported: Arib (Aïn-Defla Dept.) and Ihrir (Illizi Dept.).
Recommended prophylaxis: –.

AMERICAN SAMOA

Yellow fever – A yellow fever vaccination certificate is required from travellers over 1 year of age coming from infected areas.

ANDORRA

No vaccination requirements for any international traveller.

ANGOLA

Yellow fever – A yellow fever vaccination certificate is required from travellers over 1 year of age coming from infected areas.[1]

Malaria – Malaria risk–predominantly in the malignant *(P. falciparum)* form–exists throughout the year in the whole country. *P. falciparum* resistant to chloroquine and sulfadoxine-pyrimethamine reported.
Recommended prophylaxis: MEF.

ANTIGUA AND BARBUDA

Yellow fever – A yellow fever vaccination certificate is required from travellers over 1 year of age coming from infected areas.

ARGENTINA

No vaccination requirements for any international traveller.

Malaria – Malaria risk–almost exclusively in the benign *(P. vivax)* form–exists from October through May below 1200 m in rural areas of Iruya, Orán, San Martín and Santa Victoria Dep. (Salta Prov.), and Ledesma, San Pedro and Santa Barbara Dep. (Jujuy Prov.).
Recommended prophylaxis in risk areas: CHL.

---

[1] See pp. 10–11 and map 1, p. 14.

ARMENIA

The regulations published under "Former USSR" apply to Armenia until further notice.

AUSTRALIA

Yellow fever – A yellow fever vaccination certificate is required from travellers over 1 year of age entering Australia within 6 days of leaving an infected country, as listed in the *Weekly epidemiological record*.

AUSTRIA

No vaccination requirements for any international traveller.

AZERBAIJAN

No vaccination requirements for any international traveller.

Malaria – Malaria risk–exclusively in the benign *(P. vivax)* form–exists in southern areas, as well as in the Khachmas region in the north. There is no risk in Baku.
Recommended prophylaxis in risk areas: CHL.

BAHAMAS

Yellow fever – A yellow fever vaccination certificate is required from travellers over 1 year of age coming from infected areas.

BAHRAIN

No vaccination requirements for any international traveller.

BANGLADESH

Yellow fever – Any person (including infants) who arrives by air or sea without a certificate is detained in isolation for a period of up to 6 days if arriving within 6 days of departure from an infected area or having been in transit in such an area, or having come by an aircraft that has been in an infected area and has not been disinsected in accordance with the procedure and formulation laid down in Schedule VI of the Bangladesh Aircraft (Public Health) Rules 1977 (First Amendment) or those recommended by WHO.

The following countries and areas are regarded as infected:

Africa: Angola, Benin, Botswana, Burkina Faso, Burundi, Cameroon, Central African Republic, Chad, Congo, Côte d'Ivoire, Equatorial Guinea, Ethiopia, Gabon, Gambia, Ghana, Guinea, Guinea-Bissau, Kenya, Liberia, Malawi, Mali, Mauritania, Niger, Nigeria, Rwanda, Sao Tome and Principe, Senegal, Sierra Leone, Somalia, Sudan (south of 15° N), Togo, Uganda, United Republic of Tanzania, Zaire, Zambia.

America: Belize, Bolivia, Brazil, Colombia, Costa Rica, Ecuador, French Guiana, Guatemala, Guyana, Honduras, Nicaragua, Panama, Peru, Suriname, Trinidad and Tobago, Venezuela.

Note: When a case of yellow fever is reported from any country, that country is regarded by the Government of Bangladesh as infected with yellow fever and is added to the above list.

Malaria – Malaria risk exists throughout the year in the whole country, excluding Dhaka City. *P. falciparum* highly resistant to chloroquine and resistant to sulfadoxine–pyrimethamine reported.

Recommended prophylaxis: C+P; in forested areas and south-east, MEF.

BARBADOS

Yellow fever – A yellow fever vaccination certificate is required from travellers over 1 year of age coming from infected areas.

BELARUS

No vaccination requirements for any international traveller.

BELGIUM

No vaccination requirements for any international traveller.

BELIZE

Yellow fever – A yellow fever vaccination certificate is required from travellers coming from infected areas.

Malaria – Malaria risk–predominantly in the benign *(P. vivax)* form–exists throughout the year except in Belize Distr. and urban areas.

Recommended prophylaxis in risk areas: CHL.

BENIN

Yellow fever – A yellow fever vaccination certificate is required from all travellers over 1 year of age.

Malaria – Malaria risk–predominantly in the malignant *(P. falciparum)* form–exists throughout the year in the whole country. Chloroquine-resistant *P. falciparum* reported.

Recommended prophylaxis: MEF.

BERMUDA

No vaccination requirements for any international traveller.

BHUTAN

Yellow fever – A yellow fever vaccination certificate is required from travellers coming from infected areas.

Malaria – Malaria risk exists throughout the year in the southern belt of five districts: Chirang, Gaylegphug, Samchi, Samdrupjongkhar, Shemgang. *P. falciparum* resistant to chloroquine and sulfadoxine–pyrimethamine reported.

Recommended prophylaxis in risk areas: C+P.

BOLIVIA

Yellow fever – A yellow fever vaccination certificate is required from travellers coming from infected areas. Vaccination is recommended for incoming travellers from non-infected zones visiting risk areas such as the Departments of Beni, Chuquisaca, Cochabamba, Pando, Santa Cruz, Tarija, and part of La Paz Department.

Malaria – Malaria risk–predominantly in the benign *(P. vivax)* form–exists throughout the year below 2500 m, excluding urban areas and excluding Oruro Department, the provinces of Ingavi, Los Andes, Omasuyos, and Pacajes (La Paz Department), and Southern and Central Potosí Department. Falciparum malaria occurs in the northern departments bordering Brazil (Acre and Rondônia States), especially in the localities of Guayaramerín, Riberalta and Puerto Rico. *P. falciparum* resistant to chloroquine and sulfadoxine–pyrimethamine reported.

Recommended prophylaxis in risk areas: CHL; in northern departments, MEF.

BOSNIA AND HERZEGOVINA

The regulations published under Yugoslavia also apply to Bosnia and Herzegovina until further notice.

BOTSWANA

No vaccination requirements for any international traveller.

Malaria – Malaria risk–predominantly in the malignant *(P. falciparum)* form–exists from November to May/June in the northern parts of the country: Boteti, Chobe, Ngamiland, Okavango, Tutume districts/subdistricts. Chloroquine-resistant *P. falciparum* reported.

Recommended prophylaxis in risk areas: C+P.

BRAZIL

Yellow fever – A yellow fever vaccination certificate is required from travellers over 9 months of age coming from infected areas, unless they are in possession of a waiver stating that immunization is contraindicated on medical grounds. The following countries or areas are regarded as infected:

Africa: Angola, Cameroon, Gambia, Guinea, Kenya, Mali, Nigeria, Sudan, Zaire.

America: Bolivia, Colombia, Ecuador, Peru.

Vaccination is recommended for travellers to rural areas in Acre, Amazonas, Goiás, Maranhão, Mato Grosso, Mato Grosso do Sul, Pará, and Rondônia States and Terr. of Amapá and Roraima.

Malaria – Malaria risk exists throughout the year below 900 m in some rural areas of: Acre, Amazonas, Maranhão, Mato Grosso, Pará, Rondônia and Tocantins States, and in Terr. of Amapá and Roraima, as well as in the outskirts of Manaus and Pôrto Velho. Risk is high in areas of mining and agricultural colonization: the north and west of Mato Grosso; the south of Pará (along the highways Transamazônica and Cuiabá-Santarém, the valleys of Tapajós/Jamanxym, Araguaia/Tocantins and Xingú rivers, and in some coastal *municipios* in Salgado region); the northern half of Rondônia (*municipios* of Pôrto Velho, Ariquemes, Machadinho, Costa Marques and Candeias); the north and west of Roraima, especially the areas of the Yanomanis and Macuxís; Acre (settlement areas in the valleys of Acre, Abuná and Tarauacá rivers and along the highway Tarauacá-Cruzeiro do Sul); Amazonas State (the region of Manaus including neighbouring *municipios* and those of the lower Negro, Madeira, Purús and Solimões rivers); Amapá (northern areas and Jari river valley); Maranhão (centre of the western part); Tocantins (mainly the north and centre of Araguaia region and some isolated *municipios* of the south). In the other states outside the Amazon region, only a few local cases occur, in rural areas, originating from infection imported from the Amazon region. *P. falciparum* highly resistant to chloroquine and resistant to sulfadoxine-pyrimethamine reported.

Recommended prophylaxis in risk areas: MEF.

BRITISH VIRGIN ISLANDS

No vaccination requirements for any international traveller.

BRUNEI DARUSSALAM

Yellow fever – A yellow fever vaccination certificate is required from travellers over 1 year of age coming from infected areas or who have passed through partly or wholly endemic areas within the preceding 6 days. The countries and areas included in the endemic zones (see maps 1 and 2, pp. 14–15) are considered as infected areas.

BULGARIA

No vaccination requirements for any international traveller.

BURKINA FASO

Yellow fever – A yellow fever vaccination certificate is required from all travellers over 1 year of age.

Malaria – Malaria risk–predominantly in the malignant *(P. falciparum)* form–exists throughout the year in the whole country. Resistance to chloroquine reported.
Recommended prophylaxis: MEF.

BURMA *see* MYANMAR

BURUNDI

Yellow fever – A yellow fever vaccination certificate is required from travellers over 1 year of age coming from infected areas.[1]

Malaria – Malaria risk–predominantly in the malignant *(P. falciparum)* form–exists

throughout the year in the whole country. Resistance to chloroquine reported.
Recommended prophylaxis: MEF.

CAMBODIA

Yellow fever – A yellow fever vaccination certificate is required from travellers coming from infected areas.

Malaria – Malaria risk–predominantly in the malignant *(P. falciparum)* form–exists throughout the year in the whole country except in Phnom Penh. *P. falciparum* highly resistant to chloroquine and resistant to sulfadoxine–pyrimethamine reported. Resistance to mefloquine reported in western provinces.
Recommended prophylaxis: MEF; in western provinces, DOX.

CAMEROON

Yellow fever – A yellow fever vaccination certificate is required from all travellers over 1 year of age.

Malaria – Malaria risk–predominantly in the malignant *(P. falciparum)* form–exists throughout the year in the whole country. *P. falciparum* resistant to chloroquine and sulfadoxine–pyrimethamine reported.
Recommended prophylaxis: MEF.

CANADA

No vaccination requirements for any international traveller.

CAPE VERDE

Yellow fever – A yellow fever vaccination certificate is required from travellers over 1 year of age coming from countries having notified cases in the last 6 years.

Malaria – Limited malaria risk exists from September through November in São Tiago Island.
Recommended prophylaxis: –.

---

[1] See pp. 10–11 and map 1, p. 14.

CAYMAN ISLANDS

No vaccination requirements for any international traveller.

CENTRAL AFRICAN REPUBLIC

Yellow fever – A yellow fever vaccination certificate is required from all travellers over 1 year of age.

Malaria – Malaria risk–predominantly in the malignant *(P. falciparum)* form–exists throughout the year in the whole country. Resistance to chloroquine reported.
Recommended prophylaxis: MEF.

CHAD

Yellow fever – A yellow fever vaccination certificate is recommended for all travellers over 1 year of age.

Malaria – Malaria risk–predominantly in the malignant *(P. falciparum)* form–exists throughout the year in the whole country. Resistance to chloroquine reported.
Recommended prophylaxis: MEF.

CHILE

No vaccination requirements for any international traveller.

CHINA

Yellow fever – A yellow fever vaccination certificate is required from travellers coming from infected areas.

Malaria – Malaria risk–predominantly in the benign *(P. vivax)* form–exists principally in Guangdong, Guizhou, Yunnan, Guangxi, Hainan, Sichuan, and Fujian. Falciparum malaria occurs in Hainan and Yunnan; it is reported sporadically in Guangxi. There is generally very low malaria risk *(P. vivax* only) in Anhui, Hubei, Hunan, Jiangsu, Jiangxi, Shandong, Shanghai, and Zhejiang, although within these provinces this risk may be higher in areas of focal outbreak.

Where transmission exists, it occurs below 1500 m from July to November north of latitude 33° N, from May to December between 33° N and 25° N, and throughout the year south of 25° N.

There is no malaria risk in Heilongjiang, Jilin, Nei Monggol, Gansu, Beijing, Shanxi, Ningxia, Qinghai, Xinjiang (except along the valley of the Yili river), and Xizang (except along the valley of the Zangbo river in the extreme south-east).
Recommended prophylaxis in risk areas: CHL; in Hainan and Yunnan, MEF.

CHRISTMAS ISLAND
(Indian Ocean)

Same requirements as mainland Australia.

COLOMBIA

Yellow fever – Vaccination is recommended for travellers who may visit the following areas considered to be endemic for yellow fever: middle valley of the Magdalena river, eastern and western foothills of the Cordillera Oriental from the frontier with Ecuador to that with Venezuela, Urabá, foothills of the Sierra Nevada, eastern plains (Orinoquia) and Amazonia.

Malaria – Malaria risk exists throughout the year in rural areas below 800 m. There is high risk in the following regions: Urabá (Antioquia and Chocó Dep.), Bajo Cauca-Nechi (Antioquia and Córdoba Dep.), middle valley of the Magdalena river, Catatumbo (Norte de Santander Dep.), whole Pacific Coast area, eastern plains (Orinoquia) and Amazonia. *P. falciparum* highly resistant to chloroquine and resistant to sulfadoxine-pyrimethamine reported.
Recommended prophylaxis in risk areas: MEF.

COMOROS

No vaccination requirements for any international traveller.

Malaria – Malaria risk–predominantly in the malignant *(P. falciparum)* form–exists

throughout the year in the whole country. Resistance to chloroquine reported.
Recommended prophylaxis: MEF.

CONGO

Yellow fever – A yellow fever vaccination certificate is required from all travellers over 1 year of age.

Malaria – Malaria risk–predominantly in the malignant *(P. falciparum)* form–exists throughout the year in the whole country. Resistance to chloroquine reported.
Recommended prophylaxis: MEF.

COOK ISLANDS

No vaccination requirements for any international traveller.

COSTA RICA

No vaccination requirements for any international traveller.

Malaria – Malaria risk–almost exclusively in the benign *(P.vivax)* form–exists throughout the year in rural areas below 700 m, especially in the cantons of Matina and Central de Limón (Limón Prov.), but also in San Carlos, Los Chiles and Sarapiqué cantons.
Recommended prophylaxis in risk areas: CHL.

CÔTE D'IVOIRE

Yellow fever – A yellow fever vaccination certificate is required from all travellers over 1 year of age.

Malaria – Malaria risk–predominantly in the malignant *(P. falciparum)* form–exists throughout the year in the whole country. Resistance to chloroquine reported.
Recommended prophylaxis: MEF.

CROATIA

No vaccination requirements for any international traveller.

CUBA

No vaccination requirements for any international traveller.

CYPRUS

No vaccination requirements for any international traveller.

CZECH REPUBLIC

No vaccination requirements for any international traveller.

DEMOCRATIC PEOPLE'S REPUBLIC OF KOREA

No vaccination requirements for any international traveller.

DENMARK

No vaccination requirements for any international traveller.

DJIBOUTI

Yellow fever – A yellow fever vaccination certificate is required from travellers over 1 year of age coming from infected areas.

Malaria – Malaria risk–predominantly in the malignant *(P. falciparum)* form–exists throughout the year in the whole country. Chloroquine-resistant *P. falciparum* reported.
Recommended prophylaxis: MEF.

DOMINICA

Yellow fever – A yellow fever vaccination certificate is required from travellers over 1 year of age coming from infected areas.

DOMINICAN REPUBLIC

No vaccination requirements for any international traveller.

Malaria – Malaria risk–exclusively in the malignant *(P. falciparum)* form–exists throughout the year in Barahona Mun. and Cabral Mun. (Barahona Prov.); Dajabón Prov.; Comendador Mun. (Elias Piña Prov.); Jimaní Mun. (Independencia Prov.); Montecristi Prov.; and Pedernales Mun. (Pedernales Prov.).

Recommended prophylaxis in risk areas: CHL.

ECUADOR

Yellow fever – A yellow fever vaccination certificate is required from travellers over 1 year of age coming from infected areas.[1]

Malaria – Malaria risk–predominantly in the benign *(P. vivax)* form–exists throughout the year below 1500 m in the provinces of El Oro, Esmeraldas, Guayas, Los Ríos Manabí, Morona Santiago, Napo, Pastaza, Pichincha, Sucumbíos, and Zamora Chinchipe. Chloroquine-resistant *P. falciparum* reported.

Recommended prophylaxis in risk areas: MEF.

EGYPT

Yellow fever – A yellow fever vaccination certificate is required from travellers over 1 year of age coming from infected areas. The following countries and areas are regarded as infected areas; air passengers in transit coming from these countries or areas without a certificate will be detained in the precincts of the airport until they resume their journey:

Africa: Angola, Benin, Botswana, Burkina Faso, Burundi, Cameroon, Central African Republic, Chad, Congo, Côte d'Ivoire, Equatorial Guinea, Ethiopia, Gabon, Gambia, Ghana, Guinea, Guinea-Bissau, Kenya, Liberia, Malawi, Mali, Mauritania, Niger, Nigeria, Rwanda, Sao Tome and Principe, Senegal, Sierra Leone, Somalia, Sudan (south of 15° N), Togo, Uganda, United Republic of Tanzania, Zaire, Zambia.

America: Belize, Bolivia, Brazil, Colombia, Costa Rica, Ecuador, French Guiana, Guatemala, Guyana, Honduras, Nicaragua, Panama, Peru, Suriname, Trinidad and Tobago, Venezuela.

All arrivals from Sudan are required to possess either a vaccination certificate or a location certificate issued by a Sudanese official centre stating that they have not been in Sudan south of 15° N within the previous 6 days.

Malaria – Malaria risk–in the malignant *(P. falciparum)* and benign *(P. vivax)* forms–exists from June through October in El Faiyûm area.

Recommended prophylaxis in risk areas: CHL.

EL SALVADOR

Yellow fever – A yellow fever vaccination certificate is required from travellers over 6 months of age coming from infected areas.

Malaria – Malaria risk–almost exclusively in the benign *(P. vivax)* form–exists throughout the year in the whole country, but is greater below 600 m in the rainy season.

Recommended prophylaxis: CHL.

EQUATORIAL GUINEA

Yellow fever – A yellow fever vaccination certificate is required from travellers coming from infected areas.[2]

Malaria – Malaria risk–predominantly in the malignant *(P. falciparum)* form–exists throughout the year in the whole country. Resistance to chloroquine reported.

Recommended prophylaxis: MEF.

ERITREA

Yellow fever – A yellow fever vaccination certificate is required from travellers coming from infected areas.

Malaria – Malaria risk–predominantly in the malignant *(P. falciparum)* form–exists

---

[1] See pp. 10–11 and map 2, p. 15.

[2] See pp. 10–11 and map 1, p. 14.

throughout the year in the whole country below 2000 m.
Recommended prophylaxis: MEF.

ESTONIA

No vaccination requirements for any international traveller.

ETHIOPIA

Yellow fever – A yellow fever vaccination certificate is required from travellers over 1 year of age coming from infected areas.[1]

Malaria – Malaria risk–predominantly in the malignant *(P. falciparum)* form–exists throughout the year in the whole country below 2000 m. Highly chloroquine-resistant *P. falciparum* reported.
Recommended prophylaxis: MEF.

FALKLAND ISLANDS (MALVINAS)

No vaccination requirements for any national traveller.

FAROE ISLANDS

No vaccination requirements for any international traveller.

FIJI

Yellow fever – A yellow fever vaccination certificate is required from travellers over 1 year of age coming from infected areas.

FINLAND

No vaccination requirements for any international traveller.

FRANCE

No vaccination requirements for any international traveller.

FRENCH GUIANA

Yellow fever – A yellow fever vaccination certificate is required from all travellers over 1 year of age.

Malaria – Malaria risk exists throughout the year in the whole area. Resistance to chloroquine reported.
Recommended prophylaxis: MEF.

FRENCH POLYNESIA

Yellow fever – A yellow fever vaccination certificate is required from travellers over 1 year of age coming from infected areas.

GABON

Yellow fever – A yellow fever vaccination certificate is required from all travellers over 1 year of age.

Malaria – Malaria risk–predominantly in the malignant *(P. falciparum)* form–exists throughout the year in the whole country. Resistance to chloroquine reported.
Recommended prophylaxis: MEF.

GAMBIA

Yellow fever – A yellow fever vaccination certificate is required from travellers over 1 year of age arriving from endemic or infected areas.[1]

Malaria – Malaria risk–predominantly in the malignant *(P. falciparum)* form–exists throughout the year in the whole country. Chloroquine-resistant *P. falciparum* reported.
Recommended prophylaxis: MEF.

GEORGIA

The regulations published under "Former USSR" apply to Georgia until further notice.

---

[1] See pp. 10–11 and map 1, p. 14.

GERMANY

No vaccination requirements for any international traveller.

GHANA

Yellow fever – A yellow fever vaccination certificate is required from all travellers.

Malaria – Malaria risk–predominantly in the malignant *(P. falciparum)* form–exists throughout the year in the whole country. Resistance to chloroquine reported.

Recommended prophylaxis: MEF.

GIBRALTAR

No vaccination requirements for any international traveller.

GREECE

Yellow fever – A yellow fever vaccination certificate is required from travellers over 6 months of age coming from infected areas.

GREENLAND

No vaccination requirements for any international traveller.

GRENADA

Yellow fever – A yellow fever vaccination certificate is required from travellers over 1 year of age coming from infected areas.

GUADELOUPE

Yellow fever – A yellow fever vaccination certificate is required from travellers over 1 year of age coming from infected areas.

GUAM

No vaccination requirements for any international traveller.

GUATEMALA

Yellow fever – A yellow fever vaccination certificate is required from travellers over 1 year of age coming from countries with infected areas.

Malaria – Malaria risk–predominantly in the benign *(P. vivax)* form–exists throughout the year below 1500 m. There is high risk in the Departments of Alta Verapaz, Escuintla, Huehuetenango, Izabal, Petén, and Quiché, and moderate risk in the Departments of Baja Verapaz, Jutiapa, Retalhuleu, San Marcos, Suchitepequez and Zacapa.

Recommended prophylaxis in risk areas: CHL.

GUINEA

Yellow fever – A yellow fever vaccination certificate is required from travellers over 1 year of age coming from infected areas.[1]

Malaria – Malaria risk–predominantly in the malignant *(P. falciparum)* form–exists throughout the year in the whole country. Resistance to chloroquine reported.

Recommended prophylaxis: MEF.

GUINEA-BISSAU

Yellow fever – A yellow fever vaccination certificate is required from travellers over 1 year of age coming from infected areas, and from the following countries:[1]

Africa: Angola, Benin, Burkina Faso, Burundi, Cape Verde, Central African Republic, Chad, Congo, Côte d'Ivoire, Djibouti, Equatorial Guinea, Ethiopia, Gabon, Gambia, Ghana, Guinea, Kenya, Liberia, Madagascar, Mali, Mauritania, Mozambique, Niger, Nigeria, Rwanda, Sao Tome and Principe, Senegal, Sierra Leone, Somalia, Togo, Uganda, United Republic of Tanzania, Zaire, Zambia.

---

[1] See pp. 10–11 and map 1, p. 14.

America: Bolivia, Brazil, Colombia, Ecuador, French Guiana, Guyana, Panama, Peru, Suriname, Venezuela.

Malaria – Malaria risk–predominantly in the malignant *(P. falciparum)* form–exists throughout the year in the whole country. Chloroquine-resistant *P. falciparum* reported.

Recommended prophylaxis: MEF.

GUYANA

Yellow fever – A yellow fever vaccination certificate is required from travellers coming from infected areas and from the following countries:[1]

Africa: Angola, Benin, Burkina Faso, Burundi, Cameroon, Central African Republic, Chad, Congo, Côte d'Ivoire, Gabon, Gambia, Ghana, Guinea, Guinea-Bissau, Kenya, Liberia, Mali, Niger, Nigeria, Rwanda, Sao Tome and Principe, Senegal, Sierra Leone, Somalia, Togo, Uganda, United Republic of Tanzania, Zaire.

America: Belize, Bolivia, Brazil, Colombia, Costa Rica, Ecuador, French Guiana, Guatemala, Honduras, Nicaragua, Panama, Peru, Suriname, Venezuela.

Malaria – Malaria risk exists throughout the year in all of the interior regions including the North-West Region and areas along the Pomeroon river. Chloroquine-resistant *P. falciparum* reported.

Recommended prophylaxis in risk areas: MEF.

HAITI

Yellow fever – A yellow fever vaccination certificate is required from travellers coming from infected areas.

Malaria – Malaria risk–exclusively in the malignant *(P. falciparum)* form–exists throughout the year below 300 m in suburban and rural areas.

Recommended prophylaxis: CHL.

[1] See pp. 10–11 and map 2, p. 15.

HONDURAS

Yellow fever – A yellow fever vaccination certificate is required from travellers coming from infected areas.

Malaria – Malaria risk–predominantly in the benign *(P. vivax)* form–exists throughout the year in Departments of Atlántida, Choluteca, Colón, El Paraíso, Gracias a Dios, Valle, and Yoro, especially in rural areas.

Recommended prophylaxis in risk areas: CHL.

HONG KONG

No vaccination requirements for any international traveller.

Malaria – Malaria risk is considered not to exist in urban and most rural areas. However, occasional risk cannot be excluded in certain rural areas.

HUNGARY

No vaccination requirements for any international traveller.

ICELAND

No vaccination requirements for any international traveller.

INDIA

Yellow fever – Anyone (except infants up to the age of 6 months) arriving by air or sea without a certificate is detained in isolation for up to 6 days if that person (*i*) arrives within 6 days of departure from an infected area, or (*ii*) has been in such an area in transit (excepting those passengers and members of the crew who, while in transit through an airport situated in an infected area, remained within the airport premises during the period of their entire stay and the Health Officer agrees to such exemption), or (*iii*) has come on a ship that started from or touched at any port in a yellow fever infected area up to 30 days before its arrival in India, unless such a ship has been disinsected in accordance with the procedure laid down by WHO, or (*iv*) has come by an aircraft which has been in an infected area and has not been disinsected in accordance with the provisions laid down in the Indian Aircraft Public Health Rules, 1954, or those recommended by WHO. The following countries and areas are regarded as infected:

Africa: Angola, Benin, Burkina Faso, Burundi, Cameroon, Central African Republic, Chad, Congo, Côte d'Ivoire, Equatorial Guinea, Ethiopia, Gabon, Gambia, Ghana, Guinea, Guinea-Bissau, Kenya, Liberia, Mali, Niger, Nigeria, Rwanda, Sao Tome and Principe, Senegal, Sierra Leone, Somalia, Sudan, Togo, Uganda, United Republic of Tanzania, Zaire, Zambia.

America: Bolivia, Brazil, Colombia, Ecuador, French Guiana, Guyana, Panama, Peru, Suriname, Trinidad and Tobago, Venezuela.

Note: When a case of yellow fever is reported from any country, that country is regarded by the Government of India as infected with yellow fever and is added to the above list.

Malaria – Malaria risk exists throughout the year in the whole country excluding parts of the States of Himachal Pradesh, Jammu and Kashmir, and Sikkim. Highly chloroquine-resistant *P. falciparum* reported.
Recommended prophylaxis: C+P.

INDONESIA

Yellow fever – A yellow fever vaccination certificate is required from travellers coming from infected areas. The countries and areas included in the endemic zones (see maps 1 and 2, pp. 14–15) are considered by Indonesia as infected areas.

Malaria – Malaria risk exists throughout the year in the whole country except in Jakarta Municipality, big cities, and the main tourist resorts of Java and Bali. *P. falciparum* highly resistant to chloroquine, and resistant to sulfadoxine-pyrimethamine reported.
Recommended prophylaxis in risk areas: C+P; in Irian Jaya, MEF.

IRAN (ISLAMIC REPUBLIC OF)

No vaccination requirements for any international traveller.

Malaria – Malaria risk exists from March through November mainly in the provinces of Sistan-Baluchestan, Hormozgan and Kerman (tropical part). Chloroquine-resistant *P. falciparum* reported.
Recommended prophylaxis in risk areas: CHL; in south-east, C+P.

IRAQ

Yellow fever – A yellow fever vaccination certificate is required from travellers coming from infected areas.

Malaria – Malaria risk–exclusively in the benign (*P. vivax*) form–exists from May through November, principally in areas in the north below 1500 m (Duhok, Erbil, Ninawa, Sulaimaniya and Ta'mim Prov.) but also in Basrah Province.
Recommended prophylaxis: CHL.

IRELAND

No vaccination requirements for any international traveller.

ISRAEL

No vaccination requirements for any international traveller.

ITALY

No vaccination requirements for any international traveller

JAMAICA

Yellow fever – A yellow fever vaccination certificate is required from travellers over 1 year of age coming from infected areas.

JAPAN

No vaccination requirements for any international traveller.

JORDAN

Yellow fever – A yellow fever vaccination certificate is required from travellers coming from endemic areas in Africa.

KAZAKHSTAN

The regulations published under "Former USSR" apply to Kazakhstan until further notice.

KENYA

Yellow fever – A yellow fever vaccination certificate is required from travellers over 1 year of age coming from infected areas.[1]

Malaria – Malaria risk–predominantly in the malignant *(P. falciparum)* form–exists throughout the year in the whole country. There is normally little risk in the city of Nairobi and in the highlands (above 2500 m) of Central, Rift Valley, Eastern, Nyanza and Western Provinces. *P. falciparum* highly resistant to chloroquine and resistant to sulfadoxine–pyrimethamine reported.
Recommended prophylaxis: MEF.

KIRIBATI

Yellow fever – A yellow fever vaccination certificate is required from travellers over 1 year of age coming from infected areas.

KUWAIT

No vaccination requirements for any international traveller.

KYRGYZSTAN

The regulations published under "Former USSR" apply to Kyrgyzstan until further notice.

LAO PEOPLE'S DEMOCRATIC REPUBLIC

Yellow fever – A yellow fever vaccination certificate is required from travellers coming from infected areas.

Malaria – Malaria risk–predominantly in the malignant *(P. falciparum)* form–exists throughout the year in the whole country except in Vientiane. Highly chloroquine-resistant *P. falciparum* reported.
Recommended prophylaxis: MEF.

LATVIA

No vaccination requirements for any international traveller.

LEBANON

Yellow fever – A yellow fever vaccination certificate is required from travellers coming from infected areas.

LESOTHO

Yellow fever – A yellow fever vaccination certificate is required from travellers coming from infected areas.

LIBERIA

Yellow fever – A yellow fever vaccination certificate is required from all travellers over 1 year of age.

Malaria – Malaria risk–predominantly in the malignant *(P. falciparum)* form–exists throughout the year in the whole country. *P. falciparum* highly resistant to chloroquine and resistant to sulfadoxine–pyrimethamine reported.
Recommended prophylaxis: MEF.

---

[1] See pp. 10–11 and map 1, p. 14.

LIBYAN ARAB JAMAHIRIYA

Yellow fever – A yellow fever vaccination certificate is required from travellers over 1 year of age coming from infected areas.

Malaria – Very limited malaria risk exists in two small foci in the south-west of the country from February through August. No indigenous cases reported in recent years.

LIECHTENSTEIN

No vaccination requirements for any international traveller.

LITHUANIA

No vaccination requirements for any international traveller.

LUXEMBOURG

No vaccination requirements for any international traveller.

MACAO

No vaccination requirements for any international traveller.

MADAGASCAR

Yellow fever – A yellow fever vaccination certificate is required from travellers coming from, or having been in transit in, areas considered to be infected.

Malaria – Malaria risk–predominantly in the malignant *(P. falciparum)* form–exists throughout the year in the whole country, especially in the coastal areas. Resistance to chloroquine reported.
Recommended prophylaxis: MEF.

MALAWI

Yellow fever – A yellow fever vaccination certificate is required from travellers coming from infected areas.

Malaria – Malaria risk–predominantly in the malignant *(P. falciparum)* form–exists throughout the year in the whole country. *P. falciparum* highly resistant to chloroquine and resistant to sulfadoxine–pyrimethamine reported.
Recommended prophylaxis: MEF.

MALAYSIA

Yellow fever – A yellow fever vaccination certificate is required from travellers over 1 year of age coming from infected areas. The countries and areas included in the endemic zones (see maps 1 and 2, pp. 14–15) are considered as infected areas.

Malaria – Malaria risk exists only in limited foci in the deep hinterland. Urban and coastal areas are free from malaria, except in Sabah, where there is risk–predominantly in the malignant *(P. falciparum)* form–throughout the year. *P. falciparum* highly resistant to chloroquine and resistant to sulfadoxine–pyrimethamine reported.
Recommended prophylaxis in risk areas: C+P; in Sabah, MEF.

MALDIVES

Yellow fever – A yellow fever vaccination certificate is required from travellers coming from infected areas.

Malaria – Malaria risk disappearing; last 2 indigenous cases reported in 1983.

MALI

Yellow fever – A yellow fever vaccination certificate is required from all travellers over 1 year of age.

Malaria – Malaria risk–predominantly in the malignant *(P. falciparum)* form–exists throughout the year in the whole country. Resistance to chloroquine reported.
Recommended prophylaxis: MEF.

MALTA

Yellow fever – A yellow fever vaccination certificate is required from travellers over 9 months of age coming from infected areas. If indicated on epidemiological grounds, infants under 9 months of age are subject to isolation or surveillance if coming from an infected area.

MARSHALL ISLANDS

No vaccination requirements for any international traveller.

MARTINIQUE

Yellow fever – A yellow fever vaccination certificate is required from travellers over 1 year of age coming from infected areas.

MAURITANIA

Yellow fever – A yellow fever vaccination certificate is required from all travellers over 1 year of age, except those arriving from a non-infected area and staying less than 2 weeks in the country.[1]

Malaria – Malaria risk–predominantly in the malignant *(P. falciparum)* form–exists throughout the year in the whole country, except in the northern areas: Dakhlet-Nouadhibou and Tiris-Zemour. In Adrar and Inchiri there is malaria risk during the rainy season (July through October).
Recommended prophylaxis in risk areas: C+P.

MAURITIUS

Yellow fever – A yellow fever vaccination certificate is required from travellers over 1 year of age coming from infected areas. The countries and areas included in the endemic zones (see maps 1 and 2, pp. 14–15) are considered as infected areas.

Malaria – Malaria risk–exclusively in the benign *(P. vivax)* form–exists throughout the year in certain rural areas, except Rodrigues Island.
Recommended prophylaxis: –.

MAYOTTE
(French territorial collectivity)

No vaccination requirements for any international traveller.

Malaria – Malaria risk–predominantly in the malignant *(P. falciparum)* form–exists throughout the year.
Recommended prophylaxis: MEF.

MEXICO

Yellow fever – A yellow fever vaccination certificate is requested from travellers over 6 months of age coming from infected areas.

Malaria – Malaria risk–almost exclusively in the benign *(P. vivax)* form–exists throughout the year in some rural areas that are not often visited by tourists. The states most affected (in decreasing order of importance) are: Oaxaca, Chiapas, Sinaloa, Campeche, Quintana Roo, Nayarit, Tabasco, Michoacán, Chihuahua, Hidalgo.
Recommended prophylaxis in risk areas: CHL.

MICRONESIA
(FEDERATED STATES OF)

No vaccination requirements for any international traveller.

MONACO

No vaccination requirements for any international traveller.

MONGOLIA

No vaccination requirements for any international traveller.

MONTSERRAT

No vaccination requirements for any international traveller.

---

[1] See pp. 10–11 and map 1, p. 14.

MOROCCO

No vaccination requirements for any international traveller.

Malaria – Malaria risk–exclusively in the benign *(P. vivax)* form–exists from May to October in certain rural areas of some provinces. Limited foci are reported mainly in the following provinces (in decreasing order of importance): Beni Mellal, Taza, Khemisset, Khouribga, Khénifra, Chefchaouen, Taounate, El Kelâa Srahna, Settat, and Larache.

Recommended prophylaxis: –.

MOZAMBIQUE

Yellow fever – A yellow fever vaccination certificate is required from travellers over 1 year of age coming from infected areas.

Malaria – Malaria risk–predominantly in the malignant *(P. falciparum)* form–exists throughout the year in the whole country. *P. falciparum* highly resistant to chloroquine and resistant to sulfadoxine-pyrimethamine reported.

Recommended prophylaxis: MEF.

MYANMAR (formerly BURMA)

Yellow fever – A yellow fever vaccination certificate is required from travellers coming from infected areas. Nationals and residents of Myanmar are required to possess certificates of vaccination on their departure to an infected area.

Malaria – Malaria risk–predominantly in the malignant *(P. falciparum)* form–exists commonly below 1000 m (*a*) throughout the year in Karen State; (*b*) from March through December in Chin, Kachin, Kayah, Mon, Rakhine, and Shan States, Pegu Div., and Hlegu, Hmawbi, and Taikkyi townships of Yangon (formerly Rangoon) Div.; (*c*) from April through December in the rural areas of Tenasserim Div.; (*d*) from May through December in Irrawaddy Div. and the rural areas of Mandalay Div.; (*e*) from June through November in the rural

areas of Magwe Div., and in Sagaing Div. *P. falciparum* highly resistant to chloroquine and resistant to sulfadoxine-pyrimethamine reported.

Recommended prophylaxis: MEF.

NAMIBIA

Yellow fever – A yellow fever vaccination certificate is required from travellers coming from infected areas. The countries, or parts of countries, included in the endemic zones in Africa and South America are regarded as infected (see maps 1 and 2, pp. 14–15).

Travellers on scheduled flights that originated outside the areas regarded as infected, but who have been in transit through these areas, are not required to possess a certificate provided they remained at the scheduled airport or in the adjacent town during transit.

All passengers whose flights originated in infected areas or who have been in transit through these areas on unscheduled flights are required to possess a certificate.

The certificate is not insisted upon in the case of children under 1 year of age, but such infants may be subject to surveillance.

Malaria – Malaria risk–predominantly in the malignant *(P. falciparum)* form–exists in the northern regions from November to May/June and along the Kavango river throughout the year. Resistance to chloroquine reported.

Recommended prophylaxis in risk areas: C+P.

NAURU

Yellow fever – A yellow fever vaccination certificate is required from travellers over 1 year of age coming from infected areas.

NEPAL

Yellow fever – A yellow fever vaccination certificate is required from travellers coming from infected areas.

Malaria – Malaria risk–predominantly in the benign *(P. vivax)* form–exists throughout the year in rural areas of the Terai districts (incl. forested hills and forest areas) of Dhanukha, Mahotari, Sarlahi, Rautahat, Bara, Parsa, Rupendehi, Kapilvastu, and especially along the Indian border. Chloroquine-resistant *P. falciparum* reported.

Recommended prophylaxis in risk areas: C+P.

NETHERLANDS

No vaccination requirements for any international traveller.

NETHERLANDS ANTILLES

Yellow fever – A yellow fever vaccination certificate is required from travellers over 6 months of age coming from infected areas.

NEW CALEDONIA AND DEPENDENCIES

Cholera – Vaccination against cholera is not required. Travellers coming from an infected area are not given chemoprophylaxis, but are required to complete a form for use by the Health Service.

Yellow fever – A yellow fever vaccination certificate is required from travellers over 1 year of age coming from infected areas.

NEW ZEALAND

No vaccination requirements for any international traveller.

NICARAGUA

Yellow fever – A yellow fever vaccination certificate is required from travellers over 1 year of age coming from infected areas.

Malaria – Major risk–predominantly in the benign *(P. vivax)* form–exists from June through December in rural areas as well as in the outskirts of Bluefields, Bonanza, Chinandega, León, Puerto Cabeza, Rosita,

and Siuna towns, and areas on the shore of Lake Managua in the capital region.

Recommended prophylaxis in risk areas: CHL.

NIGER

Yellow fever – A yellow fever vaccination certificate is required from all travellers over 1 year of age and recommended for travellers leaving Niger.

Malaria – Malaria risk–predominantly in the malignant *(P. falciparum)* form–exists throughout the year in the whole country. Chloroquine-resistant *P. falciparum* reported.

Recommended prophylaxis: MEF.

NIGERIA

Yellow fever – A yellow fever vaccination certificate is required from travellers over 1 year of age coming from infected areas.[1]

Malaria – Malaria risk–predominantly in the malignant *(P. falciparum)* form–exists throughout the year in the whole country. Chloroquine-resistant *P. falciparum* reported.

Recommended prophylaxis: MEF.

NIUE

Yellow fever – A yellow fever vaccination certificate is required from travellers over 1 year of age coming from infected areas.

NORTHERN MARIANA ISLANDS

No vaccination requirements for any international traveller.

NORWAY

No vaccination requirements for any international traveller.

---

[1] See pp. 10–11 and map 1, p. 14.

OMAN

Yellow fever – A yellow fever vaccination certificate is required from travellers coming from infected areas.

Malaria – Malaria risk–predominantly in the malignant *(P. falciparum)* form–exists throughout the year in the whole country. Chloroquine-resistant *P. falciparum* reported.
Recommended prophylaxis: C+P.

PACIFIC ISLANDS, TRUST TERRITORY OF THE USA

No vaccination requirements for any international traveller.

PAKISTAN

Yellow fever – A yellow fever vaccination certificate is required from travellers coming from any part of a country in which yellow fever is endemic; infants under 6 months of age are exempt if the mother's vaccination certificate shows that she was vaccinated before the birth of the child. The countries and areas included in the endemic zones (see maps 1 and 2, pp. 14–15) are considered as infected areas.

Malaria – Malaria risk exists throughout the year in the whole country below 2000 m. Chloroquine-resistant *P. falciparum* reported.
Recommended prophylaxis: C+P.

PANAMA

Yellow fever – A yellow fever vaccination certificate is recommended for all travellers going to the Province of Darién.

Malaria – Malaria risk–predominantly in the benign *(P. vivax)* form–exists throughout the year in rural communities of Lake Boyana area and of Lake Gatún area, in Alto Chucunaque and Darién areas (Darién Prov.), and in the continental areas of San Blas (Playón Chico, Mandinga, etc.).

Chloroquine-resistant *P. falciparum* reported.
Recommended prophylaxis in risk areas: CHL.

PAPUA NEW GUINEA

Yellow fever – A yellow fever vaccination certificate is required from travellers over 1 year of age coming from infected areas.

Malaria – Malaria risk–predominantly in the malignant *(P. falciparum)* form–exists throughout the year in the whole country below 1800 m. *P. falciparum* highly resistant to chloroquine and resistant to sulfadoxine–pyrimethamine reported.
Recommended prophylaxis: MEF.

PARAGUAY

Yellow fever – A yellow fever vaccination certificate is required from travellers leaving Paraguay to go to endemic areas and from travellers coming from endemic areas.

Malaria – Malaria risk–almost exclusively in the benign *(P. vivax)* form–exists from October through May in some rural parts of Alto Paraná, Amambay, Caaguazú, Canendiyú, and San Pedro Departments.
Recommended prophylaxis in risk areas: CHL.

PERU

Yellow fever – A yellow fever vaccination certificate is required from travellers over 6 months of age coming from infected areas and is recommended for those who intend to visit rural areas of the country.

Malaria – Malaria risk–almost exclusively in the benign *(P. vivax)* form–exists throughout the year in almost all rural areas below 1500 m (coastal and inter-Andean valleys and the Amazon basin). Falciparum malaria occurs sporadically in areas bordering Bolivia (Madre de Dios River), Brazil (Yavari and Acre R.), Colombia (Putumayo R.), Ecuador (Napo R.) and in Zarumilla Prov. (Tumbes Dep.). *P. falci-*

parum resistant to chloroquine and sulfadoxine–pyrimethamine reported.

Recommended prophylaxis: CHL; in border areas, MEF.

PHILIPPINES

Yellow fever – A yellow fever vaccination certificate is required from travellers over 1 year of age arriving within 6 days from infected areas.

Malaria – Malaria risk exists throughout the year in areas below 600 m, except in the provinces of Bohol, Catanduanes, Cebu and Leyte. No risk is considered to exist in urban areas or in the plains. Highly chloroquine-resistant *P. falciparum* reported.

Recommended prophylaxis in risk areas: C+P.

PITCAIRN

Yellow fever – A yellow fever vaccination certificate is required from travellers over 1 year of age coming from infected areas.

POLAND

No vaccination requirements for any international traveller.

PORTUGAL

Yellow fever – A yellow fever vaccination certificate is required from travellers over 1 year of age coming from infected areas. The requirement applies only to travellers arriving in or bound for the Azores and Madeira. However, no certificate is required from passengers in transit at Funchal, Porto Santo and Santa Maria.

PUERTO RICO

No vaccination requirements for any international traveller.

QATAR

Yellow fever – A yellow fever vaccination certificate is required from travellers over 1 year of age coming from infected areas.

REPUBLIC OF KOREA

No vaccination requirements for any international traveller.

REPUBLIC OF MOLDOVA

The regulations published under "Former USSR" apply to the Republic of Moldova until further notice.

REUNION

Yellow fever – A yellow fever vaccination certificate is required from travellers over 1 year of age coming from infected areas.

ROMANIA

No vaccination requirements for any international traveller.

RUSSIAN FEDERATION

The regulations published under "Former USSR" apply to the Russian Federation until further notice.

RWANDA

Yellow fever – A yellow fever vaccination certificate is required from all travellers over 1 year of age.

Malaria – Malaria risk–predominantly in the malignant *(P. falciparum)* form–exists throughout the year in the whole country. *P. falciparum* highly resistant to chloroquine and resistant to sulfadoxine-pyrimethamine reported.

Recommended prophylaxis: MEF.

SAINT HELENA

No vaccination requirements for any international traveller.

SAINT KITTS AND NEVIS

Yellow fever – A yellow fever vaccination certificate is required from travellers over 1 year of age coming from infected areas.

SAINT LUCIA

Yellow fever – A yellow fever vaccination certificate is required from travellers over 1 year of age coming from infected areas.

SAINT PIERRE AND MIQUELON

No vaccination requirements for any international traveller.

SAINT VINCENT AND THE GRENADINES

Yellow fever – A yellow fever vaccination certificate is required from travellers over 1 year of age coming from infected areas.

SAMOA

Yellow fever – A yellow fever vaccination certificate is required from travellers over 1 year of age coming from infected areas.

SAN MARINO

No vaccination requirements for any international traveller.

SAO TOME AND PRINCIPE

Yellow fever – A yellow fever vaccination certificate is required from all travellers over 1 year of age, except those arriving from a non-infected area and staying less than 2 weeks in the country.[1]

---

[1] See pp. 10–11 and map 1, p. 14.

Malaria – Malaria risk–predominantly in the malignant *(P. falciparum)* form–exists throughout the year. Chloroquine-resistant *P. falciparum* reported.
Recommended prophylaxis: MEF.

SAUDI ARABIA

Yellow fever – A yellow fever vaccination certificate is required from all travellers coming from countries, any parts of which are infected.

Malaria – Malaria risk–predominantly in the malignant *(P. falciparum)* form–exists throughout the year in areas other than the Eastern, Northern and Central Provinces; the high altitude areas of Asir Province; and the urban areas of Western Province (Jeddah, Mecca, Medina, Taif). Chloroquine-resistant *P. falciparum* reported.
Recommended prophylaxis in risk areas: CHL.

SENEGAL

Yellow fever – A yellow fever vaccination certificate is required from travellers coming from endemic areas.[1]

Malaria – Malaria risk–predominantly in the malignant *(P. falciparum)* form–exists throughout the year in the whole country. There is less risk from January through June in the central western regions. Resistance to chloroquine reported.
Recommended prophylaxis: MEF.

SEYCHELLES

Yellow fever – A yellow fever vaccination certificate is required from all travellers coming from infected areas.

SIERRA LEONE

Yellow fever – A yellow fever vaccination certificate is required from travellers coming from infected areas.[1]

Malaria – Malaria risk–predominantly in the malignant *(P. falciparum)* form–exists

throughout the year in the whole country. Resistance to chloroquine reported.
Recommended prophylaxis: MEF.

SINGAPORE

Yellow fever – A yellow fever vaccination certificate is required from travellers over 1 year of age coming from infected areas. Certificates of vaccination are required from travellers over 1 year of age who, within the preceding 6 days, have been in or have passed through any country partly or wholly endemic for yellow fever. The countries and areas included in the endemic zones (see maps 1 and 2, pp. 14–15) are considered as infected areas.

SLOVAKIA

No vaccination requirements for any international traveller.

SLOVENIA

No vaccination requirements for any international traveller.

SOLOMON ISLANDS

Yellow fever – A yellow fever vaccination certificate is required from travellers coming from infected areas.

Malaria – Malaria risk exists throughout the year except in a few eastern and southern outlying islets. Chloroquine-resistant *P. falciparum* reported.
Recommended prophylaxis: MEF.

SOMALIA

Yellow fever – A yellow fever vaccination certificate is required from travellers coming from infected areas.[1]

Malaria – Malaria risk–predominantly in the malignant *(P. falciparum)* form–exists

---

[1] See pp. 10–11 and map 1, p. 14.

throughout the year in the whole country. Resistance to chloroquine reported.
Recommended prophylaxis: C+P.

SOUTH AFRICA

Yellow fever – A yellow fever vaccination certificate is required from travellers over 1 year of age coming from infected areas. The countries or areas included in the endemic zone in Africa and the Americas (see maps 1 and 2, pp. 14–15) are regarded as infected.

Malaria – Malaria risk–predominantly in the malignant *(P. falciparum)* form–exists throughout the year in the low altitude areas of the northern and eastern Transvaal and north-eastern Kwazulu/Natal as far south as the Tugela river. Resistance to chloroquine reported.
Recommended prophylaxis in risk areas: C+P.

SPAIN

No vaccination requirements for any international traveller.

SRI LANKA

Yellow fever – A yellow fever vaccination certificate is required from travellers over 1 year of age coming from infected areas.

Malaria – Malaria risk–predominantly in the benign *(P. vivax)* form–exists throughout the year in the whole country excluding the districts of Colombo, Kalutara and Nuwara Eliya. Highly chloroquine-resistant *P. falciparum* reported.
Recommended prophylaxis: C+P.

SUDAN

Yellow fever – A yellow fever vaccination certificate is required from travellers over 1 year of age coming from infected areas. The countries and areas included in the endemic zones (see maps 1 and 2, pp. 14–15) are considered as infected areas. A certificate may be required from travellers leaving Sudan.[1]

Malaria – Malaria risk–predominantly in the malignant *(P. falciparum)* form–exists throughout the year in the whole country. Highly chloroquine-resistant *P. falciparum* reported.
Recommended prophylaxis: MEF.

SURINAME

Yellow fever – A yellow fever vaccination certificate is required from travellers coming from infected areas.[2]

Malaria – Malaria risk–predominantly in the malignant *(P. falciparum)* form–exists throughout the year in the whole country excluding Paramaribo Distr. and the coastal areas north of 5° N. *P. falciparum* highly resistant to chloroquine and resistant to sulfadoxine–pyrimethamine reported.
Recommended prophylaxis in risk areas: MEF.

SWAZILAND

Yellow fever – A yellow fever vaccination certificate is required from travellers coming from infected areas.

Malaria – Malaria risk–predominantly in the malignant *(P. falciparum)* form–exists throughout the year in all low veld areas (mainly Big Bend, Mhlume, Simunye and Tshaneni). Highly chloroquine-resistant *P. falciparum* reported.
Recommended prophylaxis in risk areas: MEF.

SWEDEN

No vaccination requirements for any international traveller.

SWITZERLAND

No vaccination requirements for any international traveller.

---

[1] See pp. 10–11 and map 1, p. 14.
[2] See pp. 10–11 and map 2, p. 15.

SYRIAN ARAB REPUBLIC

Yellow fever – A yellow fever vaccination certificate is required from travellers coming from infected areas.

Malaria – Malaria risk–exclusively in the benign *(P. vivax)* form–exists from May through October in some limited foci in the northern border areas.
Recommended prophylaxis: CHL.

TAJIKISTAN

The regulations published under "Former USSR" apply to Tajikistan until further notice.

Malaria – Malaria risk–predominantly in the benign *P. vivax* form–exists in some southern border areas.
Recommended prophylaxis in risk areas: CHL.

THAILAND

Yellow fever – A yellow fever vaccination certificate is required from travellers over 1 year of age coming from infected areas. The countries and areas included in the endemic zones (see maps 1 and 2, pp. 14–15) are considered as infected areas.

Malaria – Malaria risk exists throughout the year in rural, especially forested and hilly, areas of the whole country. There is no risk in cities and the main tourist resorts (e.g. Bangkok, Chiangmai, Pattaya, Phuket). *P. falciparum* highly resistant to chloroquine and resistant to sulfadoxine-pyrimethamine reported. Resistance to mefloquine and to quinine reported from areas near the borders with Cambodia and Myanmar.
Recommended prophylaxis in risk areas: MEF; in areas near Cambodia and Myanmar borders, DOX.

THE FORMER YUGOSLAV REPUBLIC OF MACEDONIA

No vaccination requirements for any international traveller.

TOGO

Yellow fever – A yellow fever vaccination certificate is required from all travellers over 1 year of age.

Malaria – Malaria risk–predominantly in the malignant *(P. falciparum)* form–exists throughout the year in the whole country. Chloroquine-resistant *P. falciparum* reported.
Recommended prophylaxis: MEF.

TOKELAU

Same requirements as New Zealand.

TONGA

Yellow fever – A yellow fever vaccination certificate is required from travellers over 1 year of age coming from infected areas.

TRINIDAD AND TOBAGO

Yellow fever – A yellow fever vaccination certificate is required from travellers over 1 year of age coming from infected areas.

TUNISIA

Yellow fever – A yellow fever vaccination certificate is required from travellers over 1 year of age coming from infected areas.

TURKEY

No vaccination requirements for any international traveller.

Malaria – Potential malaria risk–exclusively in the benign *(P. vivax)* form–exists from March through November in the Çukurova/Amikova areas and from mid-March to mid-October in south-east Anatolia.
Recommended prophylaxis in risk areas: CHL.

TURKMENISTAN

The regulations published under "Former USSR" apply to Turkmenistan until further notice.

TUVALU

No vaccination requirements for any international traveller.

UGANDA

Yellow fever – A yellow fever vaccination certificate is required from travellers over 1 year of age coming from endemic areas.[1]

Malaria – Malaria risk–predominantly in the malignant *(P. falciparum)* form–exists throughout the year in the whole country including the main towns of Fort Portal, Jinja, Kampala, Mbale and parts of Kigezi. Resistance to chloroquine reported.
Recommended prophylaxis: MEF.

UKRAINE

The regulations published under "Former USSR" apply to Ukraine until further notice.

UNITED ARAB EMIRATES

No vaccination requirements for any international traveller.

Malaria – Malaria is not considered to be a risk in the Emirate of Abu Dhabi and the cities of Dubai, Sharjah, Ajman, and Umm al Qaiwain. There is malaria risk in the foothill areas and valleys in the mountainous regions of the northern Emirates.
Recommended prophylaxis in risk areas: C+P.

UNITED KINGDOM (with Channel Islands and Isle of Man)

No vaccination requirements for any international traveller.

---

[1] See pp. 10–11 and map 1, p. 14.

UNITED REPUBLIC OF TANZANIA

Yellow fever – A yellow fever vaccination certificate is required from travellers over 1 year of age coming from infected areas. The countries and areas included in the endemic zones (see maps 1 and 2, pp. 14–15) are considered as infected areas.[1]

Malaria – Malaria risk–predominantly in the malignant *(P. falciparum)* form–exists throughout the year in the whole country below 1800 m. *P. falciparum* highly resistant to chloroquine and resistant to sulfadoxine–pyrimethamine reported.
Recommended prophylaxis: MEF.

UNITED STATES OF AMERICA

No vaccination requirements for any international traveller.

URUGUAY

No vaccination requirements for any international traveller.

Former USSR

No vaccination requirements for any international traveller.

UZBEKISTAN

The regulations published under "Former USSR" apply to Uzbekistan until further notice.

VANUATU

No vaccination requirements for any international traveller.

Malaria – Malaria risk–predominantly in the malignant *(P. falciparum)* form–exists throughout the year in the whole country excluding Futuna Island. *P. falciparum* highly resistant to chloroquine and resistant to sulfadoxine–pyrimethamine reported.
Recommended prophylaxis: MEF.

VENEZUELA

No vaccination requirements for any international traveller.[2]

Malaria – Malaria risk–predominantly in the benign *(P. vivax)* form–exists throughout the year in rural areas in part of: Amazonas, Anzoátegui, Apure, Barinas, Bolívar, Delta Amacuro, Mérida, Monagas, Portuguesa, Sucre, Táchira, and Zulia States. Highly chloroquine-resistant *P. falciparum* reported.
Recommended prophylaxis in risk areas: MEF.

VIET NAM

Yellow fever – A yellow fever vaccination certificate is required from travellers over 1 year of age coming from infected areas.

Malaria – Malaria risk exists in the whole country–predominantly in the malignant *(P. falciparum)* form–excluding urban centres and the deltas. *P. falciparum* highly resistant to chloroquine and resistant to sulfadoxine–pyrimethamine reported.
Recommended prophylaxis: MEF.

VIRGIN ISLANDS (USA)

No vaccination requirements for any international traveller.

WAKE ISLAND

No vaccination requirements for any international traveller.

YEMEN

Yellow fever – A yellow fever vaccination certificate is required from travellers over 1 year of age coming from infected areas.

Malaria – Malaria risk–predominantly in the malignant *(P. falciparum)* form–exists throughout the year, but mainly from September through February, in the whole

---

[1] See pp. 10–11 and map 1, p. 14.

[2] See pp. 10–11 and map 2, p. 15.

country excluding Aden and airport perimeter. Resistance to chloroquine reported.
Recommended prophylaxis: C+P.

YUGOSLAVIA

No vaccination requirements for any international traveller.

ZAIRE

Yellow fever – A yellow fever vaccination certificate is required from travellers over 1 year of age.

Malaria – Malaria risk–predominantly in the malignant *(P. falciparum)* form–exists throughout the year in the whole country. Highly chloroquine-resistant *P. falciparum* reported.
Recommended prophylaxis: MEF.

ZAMBIA

Yellow fever – No vaccination requirements for any international traveller.[1]

Malaria – Malaria risk–predominantly in the malignant *(P. falciparum)* form–exists throughout the year in the whole country. Highly chloroquine-resistant *P. falciparum* reported.
Recommended prophylaxis: MEF.

ZIMBABWE

Yellow fever – A yellow fever vaccination certificate is required from travellers coming from infected areas.

Malaria – Malaria risk–predominantly in the malignant *(P. falciparum)* form–exists from November through June in areas below 1200 m and throughout the year in the Zambezi valley. Resistance to chloroquine reported.
Recommended prophylaxis: MEF.

---

[1] See pp. 10–11 and map 1, p. 14.

4. GEOGRAPHICAL DISTRIBUTION OF POTENTIAL HEALTH HAZARDS TO TRAVELLERS

This section is intended to give a broad indication of the health risks to which travellers may be exposed in various areas of the world and which they may not encounter in their usual place of residence.

In practice, to identify areas accurately and define the degree of risk likely in each of them is extremely difficult, if not impossible. For example, viral hepatitis A is ubiquitous but the risk of infection varies not only according to area but also according to eating habits; hence, there may be more risk from communal eating in an area of low incidence than from eating in a private home in an area of high incidence. Generalizations may therefore be misleading.

Another factor is that tourism is an important source of income for many countries and to label specific areas as being of high risk for a disease may be misinterpreted. However, this does not absolve national health administrations from their responsibility to provide an accurate picture of the risks from communicable diseases that may be encountered in various parts of their countries.

4.1 Africa

Northern Africa (Algeria, Egypt, Libyan Arab Jamahiriya, Morocco, and Tunisia) is characterized by a generally fertile coastal area and a desert hinterland with oases that are often foci of infections.

The *arthropod-borne diseases* are unlikely to be a major problem to the traveller, although filariasis (focally in the Nile delta), leishmaniasis, malaria, relapsing fever, Rift Valley fever, sandfly fever, typhus, and West Nile fever do occur.

Food-borne and water-borne diseases are endemic, the dysenteries and other diarrhoeal diseases being particularly common. Hepatitis A occurs throughout the area. The typhoid fevers are common in some areas. Alimentary helminthic infections, brucellosis and giardiasis are common. Echinococcosis (hydatid disease) may occur. Sporadic cases of cholera occur.

Other hazards include poliomyelitis (also a food-borne or water-borne disease). However, no cases of poliomyelitis have been reported from Algeria since 1990, from the Libyan Arab Jamahiriya since 1991, from Morocco since 1989, or from Tunisia since 1992. Trachoma, rabies, snakes and scorpions are hazards in certain areas. Schistosomiasis (bilharziasis) is prevalent both in the Nile delta area and in the Nile valley; it occurs focally elsewhere in the area.

Sub-Saharan Africa (Angola, Benin, Burkina Faso, Burundi, Cameroon, Cape Verde, Central African Republic, Chad, Comoros, Congo, Côte d'Ivoire, Djibouti, Equatorial Guinea, Eritrea, Ethiopia, Gabon, Gambia, Ghana, Guinea, Guinea-Bissau, Kenya, Liberia, Madagascar, Malawi, Mali, Mauritania, Mauritius, Mozambique, Niger, Nigeria, Réunion, Rwanda, Sao Tome and Principe, Senegal, Seychelles, Sierra Leone, Somalia, Sudan, Togo, Uganda, United Republic of Tanzania, Zaire, Zambia, and Zimbabwe). In this area, entirely within the tropics, the vegetation varies from the tropical rain forests of the west and centre to the wooded steppes of the east, and from the desert of the north through the Sahel and Sudan savannas to the moist orchard savanna and woodlands north and south of the equator.

Many of the diseases listed below occur in localized foci and are confined to rural areas. They are mentioned so that the international traveller and the medical practitioner concerned may be aware of the diseases that may occur.

Arthropod-borne diseases are a major cause of morbidity. Malaria in the severe falciparum (malignant) form occurs throughout the area, except at over 3000 metres altitude and in the islands of Mauritius, Réunion and the Seychelles. Various forms of filariasis are widespread; endemic foci of onchocerciasis (river blindness) exist in all the countries listed except in the greater part of Kenya and in Djibouti, Gambia, Mauritania, Mozambique, Somalia, Zambia, Zimbabwe, and the island countries of the Atlantic and Indian Oceans. However, onchocerciasis exists in the island of Bioko, Equatorial Guinea. Both cutaneous and visceral leishmaniasis may be found, particularly in the drier areas. Visceral leishmaniasis is on the increase in Sudan. Human trypanosomiasis (sleeping sickness), mainly in small isolated foci, is reported from all countries except Djibouti, Gambia, Mauritania, Somalia, and the island countries of the Atlantic and Indian Oceans. Relapsing fever and louse-, flea- and tick-borne typhus occur. Natural foci of plague have been reported from Angola, Kenya, Madagascar, Mozambique, Uganda, the United Republic of Tanzania, Zaire, and Zimbabwe. Tungiasis is widespread. Many viral diseases, some presenting as severe haemorrhagic fevers, are transmitted by mosquitos, ticks, sandflies, etc., which are found throughout this region. Large outbreaks of yellow fever occur periodically in the unvaccinated population.

Food-borne and water-borne diseases are highly endemic. Alimentary helminthic infections, the dysenteries and diarrhoeal diseases, including giardiasis, the typhoid fevers and hepatitis A and E are widespread. Cholera is actively transmitted in many countries in this area. Dracunculiasis occurs in isolated foci. Paragonimiasis (oriental lung fluke) has been reported from Cameroon, Gabon, Liberia, and most recently from Equatorial Guinea. Echinococcosis (hydatid disease) is widespread in animal-breeding areas.

Other diseases. Hepatitis B is hyperendemic. Poliomyelitis (also a food-borne or water-borne disease) is endemic in most countries except Cape

Verde, Comoros, Mauritius, Réunion and the Seychelles. Schistosomiasis (bilharziasis) is present throughout the area except in Cape Verde, Comoros, Djibouti, Réunion and the Seychelles. Trachoma is widespread. Among other diseases, certain, frequently fatal, arenavirus haemorrhagic fevers have attained notoriety. Lassa fever has a virus reservoir in a commonly found multimammate rat. Studies have shown that an appreciable reservoir exists in some rural areas of West Africa, and people visiting these areas should take particular care to avoid rat-contaminated food or food containers, but the extent of the disease should not be exaggerated. Ebola and Marburg haemorrhagic fevers are present, but reported only infrequently.

Epidemics of meningococcal meningitis may occur throughout tropical Africa, particularly in the savanna areas during the dry season.

Other hazards include rabies and snake bites.

Southern Africa (Botswana, Lesotho, Namibia, Saint Helena, South Africa, and Swaziland) varies physically from the Namib and Kalahari deserts to fertile plateaux and plains and to the more temperate climate of the southern coast.

Arthropod-borne diseases such as Crimean-Congo haemorrhagic fever, malaria, plague, relapsing fever, Rift Valley fever, tick-bite fever, and typhus—mainly tick-borne—have been reported from most of this area except Saint Helena, but, apart from malaria in certain areas, they are unlikely to be a major health problem for the traveller. Trypanosomiasis (sleeping sickness) may occur in Botswana and Namibia.

Food-borne and water-borne diseases are common in some areas, particularly amoebiasis and the typhoid fevers. Hepatitis A occurs in this area.

Other diseases. With the exception of an epidemic in Namibia in 1993, few cases of poliomyelitis are being reported from these countries. Hepatitis B is hyperendemic. Schistosomiasis (bilharziasis) is endemic in Botswana, Namibia, South Africa and Swaziland. Snakes may be a hazard in some areas.

4.2 The Americas

Available data suggest that transmission of poliomyelitis has been interrupted in the region of the Americas since late 1991. Wild poliovirus type 3 was imported in 1992 from the Netherlands into a religious community in Canada which refuses immunization. There is no evidence to suggest that the virus spread outside this community.

North America (Bermuda, Canada, Greenland, Saint Pierre and Miquelon, and the United States of America (with Hawaii)) extends from the Arctic to the subtropical cays of the southern USA.

The incidence of communicable diseases is such that they are unlikely to prove a hazard for the international traveller greater than that found in his or her own country. There are, of course, health risks, but in general the precautions required are minimal. Certain diseases occasionally occur, such as plague, rabies in wildlife including bats, Rocky Mountain spotted fever, tularaemia, and arthropod-borne encephalitis. Recently, rodent-borne hantavirus has been identified, predominantly in the western states of the USA. Lyme disease is endemic in the north-eastern USA and the upper Midwest. During recent years, the incidence of certain food-borne diseases, e.g. salmonellosis, has increased in some regions. Other hazards include poisonous snakes, poison ivy and poison oak. In the north, a serious hazard is the very low temperature in the winter.

In the USA, proof of immunization against diphtheria, measles, poliomyelitis, and rubella is now universally required for entry into school. In addition, the school entry requirements of most states include immunization against tetanus (47 states), pertussis (38 states), and mumps (34 states).

Mainland Middle America (Belize, Costa Rica, El Salvador, Guatemala, Honduras, Mexico, Nicaragua, and Panama) ranges from the deserts of the north to the tropical rain forests of the south-east.

Of the *arthropod-borne diseases,* malaria exists in all eight countries, but in Costa Rica and Panama it is confined to a few areas and in Mexico mainly to the west coast. Cutaneous and mucocutaneous leishmaniasis occur in all eight countries. Visceral leishmaniasis occurs in El Salvador, Guatemala, Honduras and Mexico. Onchocerciasis (river blindness) is found in two small foci in the south of Mexico and four dispersed foci in Guatemala. American trypanosomiasis (Chagas disease) has been reported to occur in localized foci in rural areas in all eight countries. Bancroftian filariasis is present in Costa Rica. Dengue fever and Venezuelan equine encephalitis may occur in all countries.

The *food-borne and water-borne diseases,* including amoebic and bacillary dysenteries and other diarrhoeal diseases, and the typhoid fevers are very common throughout the area. All countries reported cases of cholera in 1993, although the risk of contracting the disease in Belize, Costa Rica, Honduras and Panama is very low. Hepatitis A occurs throughout the area. Helminthic infections are common. Paragonimiasis (oriental lung fluke) has been reported in Costa Rica, Honduras and Panama. Brucellosis occurs in the northern part of the area. Many *Salmonella typhi* infections from Mexico and *Shigella dysenteriae* type 1 infections from mainland Middle America as a whole have been caused by drug-resistant enterobacteria.

Other diseases. Rabies in animals (usually dogs and bats) is widespread throughout the area. Snakes may be a hazard in some areas.

Caribbean Middle America (Antigua and Barbuda, Aruba, Bahamas, Barbados, British Virgin Islands, Cayman Islands, Cuba, Dominica, Dominican Republic, Grenada, Guadeloupe, Haiti, Jamaica, Martinique, Montserrat, Netherlands Antilles, Puerto Rico, Saint Kitts and Nevis, Saint Lucia, Saint Vincent and the Grenadines, Trinidad and Tobago, Turks and Caicos Islands, and the Virgin Islands (USA)). The islands, a number of them mountainous with peaks 1000–2500 m high, have an equable tropical climate with heavy rain storms and high winds at certain times of the year.

Of the *arthropod-borne diseases,* malaria occurs in endemic form only in Haiti and in parts of the Dominican Republic; elsewhere it has been eradicated. Diffuse cutaneous leishmaniasis was recently discovered in the Dominican Republic. Bancroftian filariasis occurs in Haiti and some other islands and other filariases may occasionally be found. Human fascioliasis due to *Fasciola hepatica* is endemic in Cuba. Outbreaks of dengue fever occur in the area, and dengue haemorrhagic fever has also occurred. Tularaemia has been reported from Haiti.

Of the *food-borne and water-borne diseases,* bacillary and amoebic dysenteries are common and hepatitis A is reported particularly in the northern islands. No cases of cholera had been reported in the Caribbean at the time of printing.

Other diseases. Schistosomiasis (bilharziasis) is endemic in the Dominican Republic, Guadeloupe, Martinique, Puerto Rico, and Saint Lucia, in each of which control operations are in progress, and it may also occur sporadically in other islands. Other hazards may occur from spiny seaurchins and coelenterates (corals and jellyfish) and snakes. Animal rabies, particularly in the mongoose, is reported from several islands (see pp. 58-59).

Tropical South America (Bolivia, Brazil, Colombia, Ecuador, French Guiana, Guyana, Paraguay, Peru, Suriname, and Venezuela) covers the narrow coastal strip on the Pacific Ocean, the high Andean range with numerous peaks 5000–7000 m high, and the tropical rain forests of the Amazon basin, bordered to the north and south by savanna zones and dry tropical forest or scrub.

Arthropod-borne diseases are an important cause of ill health in rural areas. Malaria (in the falciparum, malariae and vivax forms) occurs in all ten countries or areas, as do American trypanosomiasis (Chagas disease) and cutaneous and mucocutaneous leishmaniasis. There has been an increase of the latter in Brazil and Paraguay. Visceral leishmaniasis is endemic in northeast Brazil, with foci in other parts of Brazil, less frequent in Colombia and Venezuela, rare in Bolivia and Paraguay, and unknown in Peru. Endemic onchocerciasis occurs in isolated foci in rural areas in Ecuador, Venezuela, and northern Brazil. The bites of blackflies may cause unpleasant reactions. Bancroftian filariasis is endemic in parts of Brazil, Guyana and Suriname. Plague has been reported in natural foci in Bolivia, Brazil, Ecuador and Peru. Among the arthropod-borne viral diseases, jungle yellow fever may be found in forest areas in all countries except Paraguay and areas east of the Andes; in Brazil it is confined to the northern and western states. Epidemics of viral encephalitis and dengue fever occur in some countries of this area. Bartonellosis, or Oroya fever, a sandfly-borne disease, occurs in arid river valleys on the western slopes of the Andes up to 3000 m. Louse-borne typhus is often found in mountain areas of Colombia and Peru.

Food-borne and water-borne diseases are common and include amoebiasis, diarrhoeal diseases, helminthic infections, and hepatitis A. Paragonimiasis (oriental lung fluke) has been reported from Ecuador, Peru and Venezuela. Brucellosis is common and echinococcosis (hydatid disease) occurs particularly in Peru. All countries except French Guiana, Paraguay, and Suriname reported autochthonous cases of cholera in 1993.

Other diseases include rodent-borne arenavirus haemorrhagic fever in Bolivia. Hepatitis B and D (delta hepatitis) are highly endemic in the Amazon basin. The intestinal form of schistosomiasis (bilharziasis) is found in Brazil, Suriname, and north-central Venezuela.

Rabies has been reported from many of the countries in this area.

Meningococcal meningitis occurs in the form of epidemic outbreaks in Brazil.

Snakes and leeches may be a hazard in some areas.

Temperate South America (Argentina, Chile, Falkland Islands (Malvinas), and Uruguay). The mainland ranges from the Mediterranean climatic area of the western coastal strip over the Andes divide on to the steppes and desert of Patagonia in the south and to the prairies of the north-east.

The *arthropod-borne diseases* are relatively unimportant except for the widespread occurrence of American trypanosomiasis (Chagas disease). Outbreaks of malaria occur in northwestern Argentina, and cutaneous leishmaniasis is also reported from the northeastern part of the country.

Of the *food-borne and water-borne diseases,* gastroenteritis (mainly salmonellosis) is relatively common in Argentina, especially in suburban areas and among children below the age of 5 years. No cases of cholera have been reported from Uruguay. Typhoid fever is not very common in Argentina but hepatitis A and intestinal parasitosis are widespread, the latter especially in the coastal region. Taeniasis (tapeworm), typhoid fever, viral hepatitis, and echinococcosis (hydatid disease) are reported from the other countries.

Other diseases. Anthrax is an occupational hazard in the three mainland countries. Animal rabies is endemic in Argentina; it has increased in the past five years but is mainly confined to urban and suburban areas. Meningococcal meningitis occurs in the form of epidemic outbreaks in Chile. Rodent-borne haemorrhagic fever is endemic in a limited zone of the pampas and in the centre of the country.

4.3 Asia

East Asia (China, the Democratic People's Republic of Korea, Hong Kong, Japan, Macao, Mongolia, and the Republic of Korea). The area includes the high mountain complexes, the desert and the steppes of the west, and the various forest zones of the east, down to the subtropical forests of the southeast.

Among the *arthropod-borne diseases,* malaria now occurs only in China. Although reduced in distribution and prevalence, bancroftian and brugian filariasis are still reported in southern China. A resurgence of visceral leishmaniasis is occurring in China. Cutaneous leishmaniasis has been recently reported from Xinjiang, Uygur Autonomous Region. Plague may be found in

China and Mongolia. Haemorrhagic fever with renal syndrome – rodent-borne, Korean haemorrhagic fever – is endemic except in Mongolia, and epidemics of dengue fever and Japanese encephalitis may occur in this area. Mite-borne or scrub typhus may be found in scrub areas in southern China, certain river valleys in Japan, and in the Republic of Korea.

Food-borne and water-borne diseases such as the diarrhoeal diseases and hepatitis A are common in most countries. Hepatitis E is prevalent in western China. Clonorchiasis (oriental liver fluke) and paragonimiasis (oriental lung fluke) are reported in China, Japan, Macao and the Republic of Korea, and fasciolopsiasis (giant intestinal fluke) in China. Brucellosis occurs in China.

Other diseases. Hepatitis B is highly endemic. The present endemic area of schistosomiasis (bilharziasis) is in the central Chang Jiang (Yangtze) river basin in China; active foci no longer exist in Japan. Low levels of poliomyelitis morbidity are reported from China and Mongolia. Trachoma and leptospirosis occur in China. Outbreaks of meningococcal meningitis occur in Mongolia.

Eastern South Asia (Brunei Darussalam, Cambodia, Indonesia, Lao People's Democratic Republic, Malaysia, Myanmar, the Philippines, Singapore, Thailand, and Viet Nam). From the tropical rain and monsoon forests of the north-west, the area extends through the savanna and the dry tropical forests of the Indochina peninsula, returning to the tropical rain and monsoon forests of the islands bordering the South China Sea.

The *arthropod-borne diseases* are an important cause of morbidity throughout the area. Malaria and filariasis are endemic in many parts of the rural areas of all the countries or areas–except for malaria in Brunei Darussalam and Singapore, where normally only imported cases occur. Foci of plague exist in Myanmar. Plague also occurs in Viet Nam. Japanese encephalitis, dengue and dengue haemorrhagic fever can occur in epidemics in both urban and rural areas. Mite-borne typhus has been reported in deforested areas in most countries.

Food-borne and water-borne diseases are common. Cholera and other watery diarrhoeas, amoebic and bacillary dysentery, typhoid fever and hepatitis A and E may occur in all countries in the area. Among helminthic infections, fasciolopsiasis (giant intestinal fluke) may be acquired in most countries in the area; clonorchiasis (oriental liver fluke) in the Indochina peninsula; opisthorchiasis (cat liver fluke) in the Indochina peninsula, the Philippines and Thailand; and paragonimiasis in most countries. Melioidosis can occur sporadically throughout the area.

Other diseases. Hepatitis B is highly endemic. Schistosomiasis (bilharziasis) is endemic in the southern Philippines and in central Sulawesi (Indonesia) and occurs in small foci in the Mekong delta. Cases of poliomyelitis (also a food-borne or water-borne disease) continue to be reported from Cambodia, Indonesia, the Lao People's Democratic Republic, Myanmar, and Viet Nam. The incidence of poliomyelitis is low in Malaysia, the Philippines and Thailand. Trachoma exists in Indonesia, Myanmar, Thailand and Viet Nam.

Other hazards include rabies, snake bites and leeches.

Middle South Asia (Afghanistan, Armenia, Azerbaijan, Bangladesh, Bhutan, Georgia, India, Islamic Republic of Iran, Kazakhstan, Kyrgyzstan, Maldives, Nepal, Pakistan, Sri Lanka, Tajikistan, Turkmenistan, and Uzbekistan). Bordered for the most part by high mountain ranges in the north, the area extends from steppes and desert in the west to monsoon and tropical rain forests in the east and south.

Arthropod-borne diseases are endemic in all of these countries except for malaria in the Maldives. There are small foci of malaria in Azerbaijan and Tajikistan. In some of the other countries malaria occurs in urban as well as rural areas. Filariasis is common in Bangladesh, India and the south-western coastal belt of Sri Lanka. Sandfly fever is on the increase. A sharp rise in the incidence of visceral leishmaniasis has been observed in Bangladesh, India and Nepal. In Pakistan, it is mainly reported from the north (Baltistan). Cutaneous leishmaniasis occurs in Afghanistan, India (Rajasthan), the Islamic Republic of Iran, and Pakistan. There are very small foci of cutaneous and visceral leishmaniasis in Azerbaijan and Tajikistan. There is evidence that natural foci of plague exist in India and Kazakhstan. Tick-borne relapsing fever is reported from Afghanistan, India and the Islamic Republic of Iran, and typhus occurs in Afghanistan and India. Outbreaks of dengue fever may occur in Bangladesh, India, Pakistan and Sri Lanka, and the haemorrhagic form has been reported from eastern India and Sri Lanka. Japanese encephalitis has been reported from the eastern part of the area and Crimean-Congo haemorrhagic fever from the western part. Another tick-borne haemorrhagic fever has been reported in forest areas in Karnataka State in India and in a rural area of Rawalpindi District in Pakistan.

Food-borne and water-borne diseases are common throughout the area, in particular cholera and other watery diarrhoeas, the dysenteries, typhoid fever, hepatitis A and E, and helminthic infections. Large epidemics of hepatitis E can occur. Giardiasis is common in the area. Foci of dracunculiasis occur in India. Brucellosis and echinococcosis (hydatid disease) are found in many countries in the area.

Other diseases. Hepatitis B is endemic. A very limited focus of urinary schistosomiasis (bilharziasis) persists in the south-west of the Islamic Republic of Iran. Outbreaks of meningococcal meningitis have been reported in India and Nepal. Poliomyelitis (also a food-borne or water-borne disease) is widespread, except in Bhutan and the Maldives. Diphtheria outbreaks are reported from Azerbaijan, Georgia, Kazakhstan, Kyrgyzstan, Tajikistan, Turkmenistan and Uzbekistan. Trachoma is common in Afghanistan and in parts of India, the Islamic Republic of Iran, Nepal and Pakistan. Snakes and the presence of rabies in animals are hazards in most of the countries in the area.

Western South Asia (Bahrain, Cyprus, Iraq, Israel, Jordan, Kuwait, Lebanon, Oman, Qatar, Saudi Arabia, Syrian Arab Republic, Turkey, the United Arab Emirates, and Yemen). The area ranges from the mountains and steppes of the north-west to the large deserts and dry tropical scrub of the south.

The *arthropod-borne diseases*, except for malaria in certain areas, are not a major hazard for the traveller. Malaria does not exist in Kuwait and no longer occurs in Bahrain, Cyprus, Israel, Jordan, Lebanon or Qatar. Its incidence in the Syrian Arab Republic is low, but elsewhere it is endemic in certain rural areas. Cutaneous leishmaniasis is reported throughout the area; visceral leishmaniasis, although rare throughout most of the area, is common in central Iraq, in the south-west of Saudi Arabia, in the north-west of the Syrian Arab Republic, in Turkey (south-east Anatolia only) and in the west of Yemen. Murine and tick-borne typhus can occur in certain countries. Tick-borne relapsing fever may occur. Crimean-Congo haemorrhagic fever has been reported from Iraq. Limited foci of onchocerciasis are reported from Yemen.

The *food-borne and water-borne diseases* are, however, a major hazard in most countries in the area. The typhoid fevers and hepatitis A exist in all countries. Dracunculiasis is found in some of these countries. Taeniasis (tapeworm) is reported from many countries in the area. Brucellosis is widespread and there are foci of echinococcosis (hydatid disease).

Other diseases. Hepatitis B is endemic. Schistosomiasis (bilharziasis) occurs in Iraq, Saudi Arabia, the Syrian Arab Republic and Yemen. The incidence of poliomyelitis (also a food-borne or water-borne disease) is low in most countries in the area, with the exception of Turkey and Yemen. Trachoma and animal rabies are found in many of the countries.

The greatest hazards to pilgrims to Mecca and Medina are heat and water depletion if the period of the Hajj coincides with the hot season.

4.4 Europe

Northern Europe (Belarus, Belgium, Czech Republic, Denmark (with the Faroe Islands), Estonia, Finland, Germany, Iceland, Ireland, Latvia, Lithuania, Luxembourg, Netherlands, Norway, Poland, Republic of Moldova, Russian Federation, Slovakia, Sweden, Ukraine, and the United Kingdom (with the Channel Islands and the Isle of Man)). The area encompassed by these countries extends from the broadleaf forests and the plains of the west to the boreal and mixed forest to be found as far east as the Pacific Ocean.

The incidence of communicable diseases in most parts of the area is such that they are unlikely to prove a hazard to the international traveller greater than that found in his or her own country. There are, of course, health risks, but in most of the area very few precautions are required.

Of the *arthropod-borne diseases*, there are very small foci of tick-borne typhus in east and central Siberia. Tick-borne encephalitis, for which a vaccine exists, Lyme disease and Crimean-Congo haemorrhagic fever may occur throughout northern Europe. Rodent-borne haemorrhagic fever with renal syndrome is now recognized as occurring at low endemic levels in this area.

The *food-borne and water-borne diseases* reported—other than the ubiquitous diarrhoeal diseases—are taeniasis (tapeworm) and trichinellosis in parts of northern Europe, and diphyllobothriasis (fish tapeworm) from the fresh-water fish around the Baltic Sea area. *Fasciola hepatica* infection can occur. Hepatitis A occurs in the eastern European countries. Cases of cholera have been reported from some countries in the area. The incidence of certain food-borne diseases, e.g. salmonellosis and campylobacteriosis, is increasing significantly in some countries.

Other diseases. Poliomyelitis (also a food-borne or water-borne disease) continues to be reported from Belarus, the Republic of Moldova, the Russian Federation and Ukraine. An outbreak of poliomyelitis in the Netherlands in 1992–93 was confined to a religious group that refuses vaccination. Rabies is endemic in wild animals (particularly foxes) in rural areas of northern Europe excepting Finland, Iceland, Ireland, Norway, Sweden and the United Kingdom. In recent years, Belarus, the Russian Federation and Ukraine have experienced extensive epidemics of diphtheria. Diphtheria cases, mostly im-ported from these three countries, have also been reported from neighbouring countries: Estonia, Finland, Latvia, Lithuania, Poland and the Republic of Moldova.

A climatic hazard in part of northern Europe is the extreme cold in winter.

Southern Europe (Albania, Andorra, Austria, Bosnia and Herzegovina, Bulgaria, Croatia, France, Gibraltar, Greece, Hungary, Italy, Liechtenstein, Malta, Monaco, Portugal (with the Azores and Madeira), Romania, San Marino, Slovenia, Spain (with the Canary Islands), Switzerland, The Former Yugoslav Republic of Macedonia, and Yugoslavia). The area extends from the broadleaf forests in the north-west and the mountains of the Alps to the prairies and, in the south and south-east, the scrub vegetation of the Mediterranean.

Among the *arthropod-borne diseases,* sporadic cases of murine and tick-borne typhus and mosquito-borne West Nile fever occur in some countries bordering the Mediterranean littoral. Both cutaneous and visceral leish-maniasis and sandfly fever are also reported from this area. Tick-borne encephalitis, for which a vaccine exists, Lyme disease and rodent-borne haemorrhagic fever with renal syndrome may occur in the eastern and southern parts of the area.

The *food-borne and water-borne diseases*–bacillary dysentery and other diarrhoeas, and typhoid fever–are more common in the summer and autumn months, with a high incidence in the south-eastern and south-western parts of the area. Brucellosis can occur in the extreme south-west and south-east and echinococcosis (hydatid disease) in the south-east. *Fasciola hepatica* infec-tion has been reported from different countries in this area. Hepatitis A occurs in the eastern European countries. Cases of cholera have been re-ported from some countries in the area. The incidence of certain food-borne diseases, e.g. salmonellosis and campylobacteriosis, is increasing signifi-cantly in some countries.

Other diseases. Poliomyelitis (also a food-borne or water-borne disease) remains endemic in Romania and Yugoslavia. Hepatitis B is endemic in the southern part of eastern Europe (Albania, Bulgaria and Romania). Rabies in animals exists in most countries of southern Europe except Gibraltar, Malta, Monaco and Portugal.

4.5 Oceania

Australia, New Zealand and the Antarctic. In Australia the mainland has tropical monsoon forests in the north and east, dry tropical forests, savanna and deserts in the centre, and Mediterranean scrub and subtropical forests in the south. New Zealand has a temperate climate with the North Island characterized by subtropical forests and the South Island by steppe vegetation and hardwood forests.

International travellers to Australia and New Zealand will, in general, not be subjected to the hazards of communicable diseases to an extent greater than that found in their own country.

Arthropod-borne diseases (mosquito-borne epidemic polyarthritis and viral encephalitis) may occur in some rural areas of Australia. Occasional outbreaks of dengue have occurred in northern Australia in recent years.

Among the *food-borne and water-borne diseases*, amoebic meningo-encephalitis has been reported.

Other hazards. Coelenterates (corals, jellyfish) may prove a hazard to the sea-bather, and heat is a hazard in the northern and central parts of Australia.

Melanesia and Micronesia-Polynesia (American Samoa, Cook Islands, Easter Island, Fiji, French Polynesia, Guam, Kiribati, Marshall Islands, Micronesia (Federated States of), Nauru, New Caledonia, Niue, Palau, Papua New Guinea, Samoa, Solomon Islands, Tokelau, Tonga, Trust Territory of the Pacific Islands, Tuvalu, Vanuatu, and the Wallis and Futuna Islands). The area covers an enormous expanse of ocean with the larger, mountainous, tropical, and monsoon rain-forest-covered islands of the west giving way to the smaller, originally volcanic peaks and coral islands of the east.

Arthropod-borne diseases occur in the majority of the islands. Malaria is endemic in Papua New Guinea and is found as far east and south as Vanuatu. Neither malaria nor the anopheline vectors are found in Fiji or the islands to the north and as far as French Polynesia and Easter Island in the east, or in New Caledonia to the south. Filariasis is widespread but its prevalence varies. Mite-borne typhus has been reported from Papua New Guinea. Dengue fever, including its haemorrhagic form, can occur in epidemics in most islands.

Food-borne and water-borne diseases, such as the diarrhoeal diseases, typhoid fever and helminthic infections, are commonly reported. Biointoxication may occur from raw or cooked fish and shellfish. Hepatitis A occurs in this area.

Other diseases. Hepatitis B is endemic. No cases of poliomyelitis have been reported from any of these islands for more than three years. Trachoma occurs in parts of Melanesia. Hazards to bathers are the coelenterates, poisonous fish and sea snakes.

5. HEALTH RISKS AND THEIR AVOIDANCE

5.1 Incidence of the major diseases that may arise from international travel

Rare but dangerous diseases may sometimes attract attention at the expense of diseases that are considered trivial but that may often interfere with travel. Fig. 1 shows the relative incidence of certain travel-related diseases in travellers from Europe and North America.

5.2 Hazards related to the environment

5.2.1 *Travel*

In the age of jet travel, international travellers are subjected to various forms of stress that may reduce their resistance to disease: crowding, long hours of waiting, disruption of eating habits, changes in climate and time zone. These factors may in themselves provoke nausea, indigestion, extreme fatigue, and insomnia.[1]

The crossing of several time zones disrupts the sleeping and waking cycle, producing jet-lag. The time needed for complete readjustment depends on the number of zones crossed and may be a week or longer. It is advisable to schedule some periods of rest in the first few days after arrival. It may also be useful to take a short-acting sleeping pill for the first few nights after the journey. People who have to take medication according to a strict time schedule (e.g. insulin, contraceptive pill) should seek a doctor's advice.

It should be noted that, with pressurization, the oxygen level and atmospheric pressure in the cabin of an aeroplane flying at an altitude of 12 000 m are equivalent to conditions found at an altitude of 2000 m (see section 5.2.3).

Travel sickness is very rare in the case of air travel. However, people travelling by boat—especially small boat—who have no experience of sea travel would be wise to take supplies of an anti-seasickness drug. Travel-sickness drugs and other medicines that need to be taken regularly should be carried as hand baggage rather than as registered luggage.

---

[1] See also section 5.8, "Special situations", pp. 83–87.

Figure 1. Estimated monthly incidence of health problems per 100 000 travellers to tropical areas

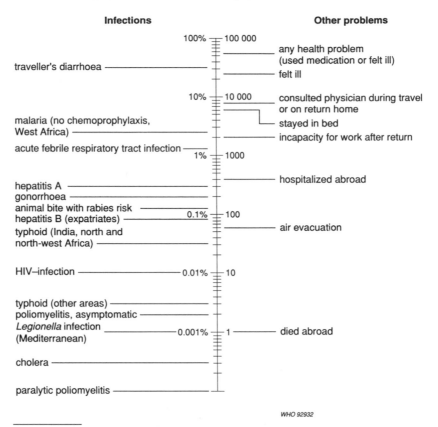

Source: Steffen R, Lobel HO. Travel medicine. In: Cook GC, ed., *Manson's tropical diseases*, 20th ed. London, WB Saunders, in press.

5.2.2 Bathing

Fresh water

Eye, ear, and intestinal infections may be contracted from polluted water. In the tropics, watercourses, canals, lakes, etc. may be infested with larvae that can penetrate the skin and cause schistosomiasis (bilharziasis). Bathing and washing in waters likely to be infested with the snail host of this parasite or contaminated with human and animal excreta should be avoided. Only swimming pools containing chlorinated water may be considered safe for bathing.

Swimming, fishing and walking barefoot in rivers or watery rice paddies, or on muddy land, may expose travellers to leptospirosis infections, especially in south-east Asia and the western Pacific regions.

"Swimmer's itch" or cercarial dermatitis due to a wide range of trematodes may be acquired in freshwater bodies of both temperate and tropical zones. These cercariae penetrate the skin and die, causing a localized or extended cutaneous allergic reaction. Treatment is symptomatic.

Sea water

Bathing in the sea does not in principle involve any risk of communicable disease. Travellers are nevertheless recommended to ascertain from local sources whether bathing is permitted and presents any hazards for health. Jellyfish stings may cause severe pain and skin irritation. In some areas, bathers should wear shoes as a protection against biting and stinging fish, coral dermatitis, and poisonous fish, shellfish and sea anemones.

Bare feet

In areas of known risk, footwear should be worn on land as a protection against ancylostomiasis, strongyloidiasis, certain mycetomas, and tungiasis.

5.2.3 Altitude

Travelling and staying at high altitudes may initially give rise to insomnia and may be distressing and even dangerous for people with cardiac or pulmonary conditions. At high altitudes there is a risk of acute pulmonary oedema and cerebral oedema, which may produce a sensation of extreme faintness, accompanied by difficulty in breathing, dizziness, headaches and vomiting. Gradual adjustment by stages and treatment with diuretics may sometimes be beneficial. Recovery follows rapidly on return to a lower altitude.

5.2.4 Heat and humidity

Excessive heat and humidity, or overexertion in these conditions, may lead to exhaustion from loss of water and salts and to severe heat-stroke requiring emergency medical attention. Tea and drinks rich in mineral salts (fruit and vegetable juices, clear soups, etc.) are recommended in cases of exhaustion. Unless contraindicated, the addition of a little table salt to food or drinks helps to prevent heat exhaustion, especially during the period of acclimatization.

Children and overweight people often suffer from skin irritation (prickly heat). Fungal skin infections such as tinea pedis (athlete's foot) are often exacerbated by heat and humidity. Daily showering, loose cotton clothing and the application of talcum powder to sensitive skin areas will help to reduce these conditions.

There can be considerable differences between day and night temperatures at any altitude. It is cool in air-conditioned rooms and aircraft. Sharp contrasts in temperature may increase susceptibility to colds, which can be prevented by dressing appropriately.

5.2.5 *Sun*

Exposure to the ultraviolet radiation of the sun can produce severe and very debilitating sun-stroke in light-skinned people. Travellers can adjust safely by gradually increasing the periods of exposure, wearing a hat and sun-glasses, and using a filter sun cream.

5.2.6 *Insects*

Many arthropods transmit communicable diseases such as: malaria (*Anopheles* mosquitos); yellow fever, dengue and dengue haemorrhagic fever (*Aedes, Haemagogus* and *Sabethes* mosquitos); viral encephalitides (*Culex* and *Anopheles* mosquitos, ticks), including Japanese encephalitis (in China, India, Japan, Lao People's Democratic Republic, Myanmar, Nepal, Philippines, Republic of Korea, Sri Lanka, Thailand, Viet Nam); filariasis (*Aedes, Anopheles, Culex* and *Mansonia* mosquitos); onchocerciasis (black-flies); leishmaniasis (sandflies); African trypanosomiasis (tsetse flies); American trypanosomiasis or Chagas disease (kissing bugs); plague and tungiasis (fleas); typhus (fleas, lice, mites, ticks); relapsing fever (lice and ticks); and Lyme disease (Lyme borreliosis) (ticks). The bites and stings of, and contact with, some arthropods can also cause unpleasant and even dangerous reactions; examples are blister beetles, fleas, mites (chiggers), bed-bugs, scorpions and spiders. On the other hand, some arthropods can bite and transmit disease without the victim being aware of the bite.

There is no evidence that the human immunodeficiency virus (HIV), the causative agent of acquired immunodeficiency syndrome (AIDS), is transmitted by insects.

There have been no reports of plague epidemics in recent years; only sporadic cases have occurred in hunters of wild rodents and in residents of remote Andean villages living in rat-infested housing.

Measures for the prevention of insect bites are described in Box 5.2, p. 73.

5.2.7 *Other animals*

Animals in general tend to avoid human beings; but they may attack, particularly if with their young.

In areas of endemic rabies, domestic dogs and cats should not be petted and contact with wild animals, especially bats, jackals, foxes, skunks, raccoons, and mongooses, as well as domestic and wild monkeys, should be avoided. Travellers should find out which animals are most likely to be rabies carriers in the area to be visited. Rabies-infected animals may be encountered in all countries. According to data available in 1992, the following countries and areas were free of rabies at that date: Australia, Bahrain, Bermuda, many of the Caribbean islands (but not, for example, Cuba and Haiti), China (Province of Taiwan), Cyprus, Denmark, Finland, Gibraltar,

Greece, Iceland, parts of Indonesia (e.g., Bali), Ireland, Japan, Kuwait, Malta, New Zealand, Norway (except the islands of Svalbard), the Pacific Islands, Papua New Guinea, Portugal, continental Spain, Sweden, the United Kingdom, and some islands of the Indian Ocean (e.g., Mauritius, Réunion, Seychelles). Travellers should find out from travel agencies and embassies the current rabies status of the area they plan to visit. No animal bite should be ignored, however, and after cleansing of the wound with antiseptic or soap, a competent opinion should be sought as to the possibility of rabies in the area.

Pre-exposure immunization may be offered to people who are: (*a*) working (even for a short time) in a rabies-infected country, if their activities may involve exposure to some special risk; (*b*) spending time (e.g. 1 month or more) in a foreign country where rabies is a constant threat; or (*c*) travelling in such a country, for any length of time, far away from a major medical centre, under special conditions (trekking, hiking). Pre-exposure immunization does not eliminate the need for prompt administration of rabies prophylaxis following contact with a suspect or rabid animal; it simply reduces the number of vaccine doses required in the post-exposure regimen. Immunoglobulin should not be used in people who have had pre-exposure immunization.

A booster dose of tetanus toxoid is recommended after an animal bite or wound and is in any case advisable every ten years under normal conditions. This precaution is especially important for campers or visitors to rural areas.

Accompanying animals (dogs and, for some countries, cats) must be immunized against rabies before they are allowed to cross international frontiers. A number of rabies-free countries also require a period of quarantine (e.g., Australia, New Zealand, United Kingdom) or a vaccination certificate together with a positive virus-neutralizing antibody test (e.g., Finland, Norway, Sweden). Before taking an animal abroad, the owner should ascertain the exact veterinary requirements of the countries of destination and of transit.

Snakes bite as a defensive reaction, particularly at night. The wearing of closed shoes or boots, recommended as a protection against mosquito and other insect bites, is a sensible precaution when walking outdoors at night in snake-infested areas. Shoes and clothing should be examined before use– particularly in the morning–as snakes and scorpions tend to rest in them. There are antivenoms to most snake poisons, but these may not be readily available in all areas.

Leather goods made from inadequately treated skins may contain anthrax spores and cause serious skin lesions.

In areas where haemorrhagic fevers or plague are endemic, contact with rodents (mice, rats) should be avoided.

5.2.8 *Accidents*

Traffic accidents are the leading cause of death among travellers. A traffic accident in an area that is not well served medically is more likely to be fatal. Regulations governing traffic and vehicle maintenance vary considerably from one country to another. Travellers using the roads should find out in advance about the state of the roads and the possibilities of fuel supply. In particular, those hiring vehicles should check carefully the insurance conditions, as well as the state of the tyres, safety belts, spare wheel, lights, brakes, etc.

5.3 Risks from food and drink

5.3.1 General considerations

"Be careful what you eat" is common advice to travellers, but very few truly understand its implications. Detailed advice on the general principles of food safety is of crucial importance to travellers.

Diarrhoea affects an estimated 20–50% of all travellers. It may cause anything from embarrassment and inconvenience to misery and disruption of travel and business plans. For vulnerable people it may even be fatal, sometimes within a few hours, if not promptly and effectively treated. Besides those that cause diarrhoea, other diseases that may be acquired by travellers from food and water include typhoid and paratyphoid fevers, poliomyelitis, viral hepatitis A and various parasitic infections.

Contaminated food and drink are the most common sources of these infections. Table 1 lists the most important agents of disease that may be present in contaminated food and water. Careful selection and preparation of food and drink offer the best protection; unfortunately, the appearance of food is no guide as to its safety and contaminated food can appear appetizing. Eating safely when travelling means not always being able to eat when, where and what one wishes. The main personal precaution is to consider unpasteurized milk, non-bottled drinks and uncooked food, apart from fruit and vegetables that can be peeled or shelled, as likely to be contaminated and therefore possibly unsafe. Similarly, dishes containing raw or undercooked eggs, such as home-made mayonnaise, some sauces (e.g. hollandaise) and some desserts (e.g. mousses), may be dangerous. Ice-cream from unreliable sources is frequently contaminated and constitutes a danger. Even with cooked food, the traveller should ensure that it has been thoroughly and freshly cooked, i.e., that it is piping hot. Foods that are cooked in advance need to be held at a temperature of below 10 °C or above 60 °C to ensure their safety. Cooked food held at ambient temperatures (15–40 °C) for some time (more than 4–5 hours) constitutes one of the greatest risks of food-borne disease, since contaminating or surviving bacteria may multiply in it. Unpasteurized milk should be boiled before it is drunk. Drinking-water should be boiled or chlorinated and filtered, except if its purity can be ensured. Ice should be avoided unless made from pure water. Beverages such as wine or beer, hot tea or coffee, and carbonated soft drinks or fruit juices that are bottled or otherwise packaged are usually safe to drink. The use of slow-release disinfectant agents in water or of filter attachments to domestic taps, if proven to give safe and reliable disinfection, may be considered.

Table 1. Some agents of important food-borne diseases and salient epidemiological features [a]

Agents	Important reservoir/carrier	Transmission [b] by			Multiplication in food	Examples of some incriminated foods
		water	food	person-to-person		
BACTERIA						
Bacillus cereus	Soil	–	+	–	+	Cooked rice, cooked meats, vegetables, starchy puddings
Brucella spp	Cattle, goats, sheep	–	+	–	+	Raw milk, dairy products
Campylobacter jejuni	Chickens, dogs, cats, cattle, pigs, wild birds	+	+	+	–[c]	Raw milk, poultry
Clostridium botulinum	Soil, mammals, birds, fish	–	+	–	+	Fish, meat, vegetables (home preserved), honey
Clostridium perfringens	Soil, animals, man	–	+	–	+	Cooked meat and poultry, gravy, beans
Escherichia coli						
Enterotoxigenic	Man	+	+	+	+	Salad, raw vegetables
Enteropathogenic	Man	+	+	+	+	Milk
Enteroinvasive	Man	+	+	0	+	Cheese
Enterohaemorrhagic	Cattle, poultry, sheep	+	+	+	+	Undercooked meat, raw milk, cheese
Listeria monocytogenes	Environment	+	+	–[c]	+	Cheese, raw milk, coleslaw
Mycobacterium bovis	Cattle	–	+	–	–	Raw milk
Salmonella typhi and paratyphi	Man	+	+	±	+	Dairy products, meat products, shellfish , vegetable salads
Salmonella (non-typhi)	Man and animals	±	+	±	+	Meat, poultry, eggs, dairy products, chocolate
Shigella spp	Man	+	+	+	+	Potato/egg salads
Staphylococcus aureus (enterotoxins)	Man	–	+	–	+	Ham, poultry and egg salads, cream-filled bakery products, ice-cream, cheese
Vibrio cholerae 01	Man, marine life	+	+	±	+	Salad, shellfish
Vibrio cholerae, non-01	Man, marine life	+	+	±	+	Shellfish
Vibrio parahaemolyticus	Seawater, marine life	–	+	–	+	Raw fish, crabs and other shellfish
Vibrio vulnificus	Seawater, marine life	+	+	–	+	Shellfish
Yersinia enterocolitica	Water, wild animals, pigs, dogs, poultry	+	+	–	+	Milk, pork, poultry
VIRUSES						
Hepatitis A virus	Man	+	+	+	–	Shellfish, raw fruit and vegetables
Norwalk agents	Man	+	+	–	–	Shellfish, salad
Rotavirus	Man	+	+	+	–	0
PROTOZOA						
Cryptosporidium parvum	Man, animals	+	+	+	–	Raw milk, raw sausage (non-fermented)
Entamoeba histolytica	Man	+	+	+	–	Vegetables, fruits
Giardia lamblia	Man, animals	+	±	+	–	Vegetables, fruits
Toxoplasma gondii	Cats, pigs	0	+	–	–	Undercooked meat, raw vegetables
HELMINTHS						
Ascaris lumbricoides	Man	+	+	–	–	Soil-contaminated food
Clonorchis sinensis	Freshwater fish	–	+	–	–	Undercooked/raw fish
Fasciola hepatica	Cattle, goats	±	+	–	–	Watercress
Opisthorchis viverrini/felineus	Freshwater fish	–	+	–	–	Undercooked/raw fish
Paragonimus spp	Freshwater crabs	–	+	–	–	Undercooked/raw crabs
Taenia saginata and T. solium	Cattle, swine	–	+	–	–	Undercooked meat
Trichinella spiralis	Swine, carnivores	–	+	–	–	Undercooked meat
Trichuris trichiura	Man	0	+	–	–	Soil-contaminated food

[a] Adapted from WHO Technical Report Series, No.705, 1984 (*The role of food safety in health and development*: report of a Joint FAO/WHO Expert Committee on Food Safety).

[b] Almost all acute enteric infections show increased transmission during the summer and/or wet months, except infections due to rotavirus and *Yersinia enterocolitica*, which show increased transmission in cooler months.

[c] Under certain circumstances some multiplication has been observed. The epidemiological significance of this observation is not clear.

+ = Yes.

± = Rare.

– = No.

0 = No information.

Travellers should always remember the popular advice: "Cook it, peel it or leave it." Before travelling, they should make sure their medical kit contains oral rehydration salts (see 5.3.2). If they expect to face situations where safe drinking-water is not available, they should also take with them water disinfectant agents.

At certain times of the year, various species of fish and shellfish contain poisonous biotoxins even if well cooked. Advice should be sought from local public health authorities on these dangerous species.

Where there is no alternative to unsafe food, smaller quantities might reduce the risk: the gastric acid has some protective effect (hypochlorhydric and achlorhydric persons are more susceptible). Travellers might also consider missing a meal–many can afford to lose a little weight and it is better to do so from choice rather than through illness.

The above advice is of particular importance for vulnerable groups, i.e. infants and children, pregnant women, the elderly, and people with suppressed immune systems.[1]

5.3.2 Diarrhoea

Diarrhoea is by far the commonest cause of ill health in travellers. No vaccine is capable of conferring general protection against diarrhoea, which has many different causes. Reliance cannot be placed on the cholera vaccine, since it offers only limited protection of a short duration; no currently available vaccine is effective against cholera and no country requires proof of cholera vaccination as a condition for entry (see section 2.3, p. 10). The injectable inactivated whole-cell vaccine against typhoid fever confers a certain amount of protection, but can have unpleasant side-effects. However, the new injectable Vi polysaccharide vaccine, given in one injection, is well tolerated and provides good protection. A booster dose is recommended every three years, and possibly more often for travellers to places where conditions of hygiene are poor. To reduce the risk of infection, travellers must take great care about what they eat and drink.

Prophylaxis of traveller's diarrhoea with bismuth subsalicylate is impractical; it is difficult to recommend an effective antibiotic for prophylaxis without knowing the type and nature of the likely causative agents in the areas to be visited. Moreover, prophylactic use of antibiotics can lead to the development of drug resistance in the agents of disease and these drugs are not without side-effects (including diarrhoea). If used at all, they should be restricted to adults with medical problems (e.g., those who take antacids) spending up to three weeks in areas where clean food and water cannot be

---

[1] The advice given in this section on how to eat safely, as well as what to do in case of diarrhoea, is summarized in a leaflet entitled A guide on safe food for travellers, which is available in Arabic, English, French, German and Spanish language editions. Public health authorities, travel agencies, transport companies, and others interested in preventing travel-related diseases are invited to distribute this leaflet. Packages of 50 copies, or a camera-ready copy, can be purchased from Distribution and Sales, World Health Organization, 1211 Geneva 27, Switzerland.

obtained, or when it is important that the travel should not be disrupted (e.g., for sporting events, diplomatic missions).

Travellers should be aware of the importance of countering the dehydration consequent upon diarrhoea by drinking plenty of fluids, preferably a rehydration fluid containing salt and glucose.[1] Dehydration can be dangerous at any age but is particularly so in small children. Cholera can cause extremely rapid and large losses of water and salts through profuse vomiting and diarrhoea, even in adults. For these cases, oral rehydration to replace salt and water losses must be particularly quick and abundant; in severe cases medical care should be sought since intravenous therapy may be required.

Antidiarrhoeal preparations, including antimotility drugs, can provide an adult with symptomatic relief; however, they can also cause undesirable side-effects and an authoritative opinion should be sought before they are used. They should never be used by children. Bacterial dysentery, protozoal infections and intestinal helminthic infections require specific treatment.

5.3.3 Viral hepatitis types A and E

Hepatitis A, formerly called infectious hepatitis, is the most common vaccine-preventable infection of travellers. Although the disease is rarely fatal, most infected persons become quite ill and many are unable to work for several weeks or months. Hepatitis A may be acquired from faecally contaminated food or water, or from direct contact with infected individuals; person-to-person transmission is particularly common between children, and between sexual partners.

Travellers from industrialized countries are likely to be susceptible to infection with hepatitis A virus (HAV), and should receive prophylactic immunoglobulin or the new hepatitis A vaccine before travelling to areas outside Australia, Canada, western Europe, Japan, New Zealand, and the USA. While people travelling to rural areas of developing countries are at particularly high risk of infection, most cases actually occur among people staying in resorts and middle- and upper-level hotels. People born and raised in developing countries, and those born before 1945 in industrialized countries, have usually been infected in childhood, and are likely to be immune. For such individuals, it may be cost-effective to test for anti-HAV antibodies in order to avoid unnecessary immunization.

Immunoglobulin has been used for over 40 years to protect against hepatitis A infection. It is safe and highly effective if given before or within 14 days of exposure. The protection provided is immediate but relatively short-lived (approximately one month per ml), so frequent travellers and those living abroad for prolonged periods require repeated injections.

A safe and highly effective inactivated (killed) HAV vaccine became available in several European countries in 1992, and widespread distribution

---

[1] The recommended composition is, for 1 litre of clean drinking-water (boiled and cooled before mixing if there is any doubt): 3.5 g sodium chloride, 2.9 g trisodium citrate dihydrate (or 2.5 g sodium bicarbonate), 1.5 g potassium chloride, 20 g glucose (or 40 g sucrose).

is expected over the next few years. Antibodies induced by the vaccine are not detectable until two weeks after administration, but reach much higher levels than those obtained with immunoglobulin. Ideally, two doses of vaccine, two weeks to one month apart, should be given before travel, with a third dose 6–12 months later. Such a schedule is expected to provide at least 10 years' protection. For travellers who seek medical advice less than two weeks before travelling, one dose of vaccine given immediately prior to the travel is likely to afford protection, but research to confirm this is not yet complete. Some clinicians give a double dose to such people; this induces antibodies in over 90% of individuals within 2 weeks, and will almost certainly protect against infection. Other clinicians give a dose of immunoglobulin with the first dose of vaccine.

Hepatitis E, formerly called enterically transmitted non-A, non-B hepatitis, is a water-borne infection, and is found in epidemics and sporadic cases. The virus has been isolated from hepatitis epidemics in Afghanistan, Bangladesh, western China, Eritrea, Ethiopia, India, Indonesia, the Islamic Republic of Iran, Kenya, Mexico, Myanmar, Nepal, Pakistan, Somalia, Sudan, and the Asian republics of the former USSR. It is probably widespread in Asia, north and sub-Saharan Africa, and the eastern Mediterranean area. The disease primarily affects young adults, is clinically similar to hepatitis A, and does not lead to chronic disease. However, among women in the second or third trimester of pregnancy who contract the disease, about 15–20% will die of fulminant hepatitis. There is no vaccine against hepatitis E, and immunoglobulin prepared in Europe or the USA does not give protection. As for many other enteric infections, avoidance of contaminated food and water is the only effective protective measure.

5.4   Sexually transmitted infections, including HIV (AIDS)

An estimated 250 million episodes of sexually transmitted infection–including human immunodeficiency virus (HIV), syphilis, genital herpes, gonorrhoea and others–occur annually throughout the world. They are important causes of infertility, illness and death. None the less, some travellers continue to place themselves at risk of infection. In a few developed countries, a large proportion of sexually transmitted infections are now acquired during international travel.

Infection with HIV, which causes AIDS, is present in virtually all countries of the world and epidemic in many of them. It is estimated that more than 17 million men, women and children have already become infected.

In addition to transmission through sexual intercourse (both heterosexual and homosexual–anal, vaginal or oral), most of these infections can be passed on from an infected mother to her unborn or newborn baby, and some–especially HIV, hepatitis B[1] and syphilis–are also transmitted through blood or blood products[2] and contaminated needles.

---

[1] See also section 5.4.2, "Hepatitis B", pp. 66–67.
[2] See also section 6.1, "Blood transfusion", p. 89.

There is no risk of acquiring any sexually transmitted infection from casual day-to-day contact at home, at work or socially. People run no risk of infection when sharing any means of communal transport (e.g. car, train, bus, aeroplane, boat) with infected persons. There is no evidence that HIV or other sexually transmitted infections are acquired from insect bites.

Measures for preventing sexually transmitted infections are the same whether the individual is travelling abroad or not, i.e. travellers should avoid sex altogether or limit it to a single faithful, uninfected partner. Intercourse with multiple partners or with persons who have multiple partners (e.g. male or female prostitutes) can be dangerous. Do not judge by appearance: most infected people look healthy and have no symptoms of disease, yet are highly infectious. If in doubt, men should always use a condom, each time, from start to finish, and women should make sure their partner uses one. Women can also protect themselves from sexually transmitted infections by using a female condom–essentially, a vaginal pouch–which is now commercially available in some countries. Hepatitis B is the only sexually transmitted infection for which there is a protective vaccine (p. 83).

The bacterial infections (e.g. gonorrhoea, syphilis, chlamydia, chancroid) can be treated, but there is no single antimicrobial that is effective against more than one or two of them. Moreover, throughout the world, many of these bacteria are showing increased resistance to penicillin and other antimicrobials. For the sexually transmitted viral infections (hepatitis B,[1] genital herpes, genital warts), treatment is inadequate or nonexistent. The same is true of HIV infection, which in its late stage causes AIDS and is thought to be invariably fatal.

To reduce the risk of acquiring HIV, hepatitis B,[1] syphilis and other infections from needles and blood, travellers should avoid injecting drugs for nonmedical purposes, and particularly any type of needle-sharing. Medical injections using unsterilized equipment are also a possible source of infection. If an injection is essential, the traveller should try to ensure that the needles and syringes come from a sterile package or have been sterilized properly by steam or boiling water for 20 minutes. Patients under medical care who require frequent injections (e.g. diabetics) should carry sufficient sterile needles and syringes for the duration of their trip and a doctor's authorization for their use.

Unsterile dental and surgical instruments, needles used in tattooing and acupuncture, ear-piercing devices, and other skin-piercing instruments can likewise transmit infection. If a blood transfusion is essential, the traveller should request blood that has been screened for HIV, hepatitis B[1] and syphilis.

Some countries have adopted HIV/AIDS-related entry restrictions and people who are infected with HIV should consult their personal physician for a detailed assessment and advice prior to travel. WHO has taken the position that there is no public health justification for entry restrictions that discriminate solely on the basis of a person's HIV status (see also p. 9).

---

[1] See also section 5.4.2, "Hepatitis B", pp. 66–67.

5.4.1 *Immunization of HIV-infected individuals*

Yellow fever. Yellow fever vaccine is recommended for travel to countries designated as yellow fever endemic zones (pp. 14–15). However, it is recognized that the risk of yellow fever infection for international travellers is low, particularly for those who limit their travel to urban areas.

Yellow fever vaccine is recommended for HIV-seropositive individuals who are asymptomatic. There is insufficient evidence to permit a definitive statement on whether administration of yellow fever vaccine poses a risk for symptomatic HIV-infected persons, and the issue is currently under investigation. Any adverse reactions to yellow fever vaccine occurring in HIV-positive individuals should be reported to WHO.

Since yellow fever is transmitted by mosquitos, the risk of infection can be reduced by taking general measures to prevent or reduce mosquito bites, including avoiding being outdoors at dusk and in the early evening, wearing long trousers and long-sleeved shirts, using mosquito repellents on exposed skin, and sleeping in screened rooms or under netting (p. 73).

Childhood immunization. Available experience suggests that the likelihood of successful immunization is reduced in some HIV-infected children but that the risk of serious adverse effects remains low. Consequently, in countries where the target diseases of the Expanded Programme on Immunization (EPI) are considered a problem, asymptomatic HIV-infected children should be immunized according to standard schedules. This also applies to children with clinical (symptomatic) AIDS, with the exception of BCG vaccine, which is safe for use in those with symptomless HIV infection, but should not be used in those who have symptoms.

5.4.2 *Hepatitis B*

Hepatitis B is highly endemic in all of Africa, much of South America, Eastern Europe, the eastern Mediterranean area, south-east Asia, China, and the Pacific Islands except Australia, New Zealand and Japan. In most of these areas, 5–15% of the population are chronically infected carriers of the hepatitis B virus (HBV), and in some areas may also carry the hepatitis D virus (delta hepatitis), which may lead to severe liver damage. Adults infected with HBV usually acquire acute hepatitis B and recover, but 5–10% develop the chronic carrier state. Infected children rarely develop acute disease, but 25–90% become chronic carriers. Approximately 25% of carriers will die from cirrhosis or primary liver cancer.

Hepatitis B may be transmitted to visitors and expatriate residents in endemic areas in a number of ways. Sexual transmission is highly efficient, as is percutaneous transmission from needle-sharing, blood transfusion, injections or other invasive procedures with unsterile medical or dental equipment, traditional medical procedures such as acupuncture, or tattooing. Medical personnel working in endemic areas are at especially high risk. Child-to-child transmission is very common.

Hepatitis B vaccines produced from plasma or by recombinant DNA technology (usually in yeast) are available and are safe and effective. Three doses of vaccine constitute the complete series; the first two doses are usually given one month apart, with the third dose 1–12 months later. Immunization will provide protection for at least 10 years. Because of the prolonged incubation period of hepatitis B, protection will be afforded to most travellers even if only the first dose is given prior to travel, provided that the subsequent doses are given upon return. Prevaccination screening to determine immune status is generally not cost-effective in people from industrialized countries, but may be in people from developing countries who have a high probability of having had asymptomatic infection during childhood.

Hepatitis B vaccine is strongly recommended for:

- all health care personnel;
- frequent travellers to endemic areas;
- persons living in endemic areas for more than 6 months;
- young children who will be in day-care or residential settings with other children in endemic areas;
- travellers likely to engage in sexual or needle-sharing activities while abroad;
- travellers who may need to undergo medical or dental procedures while abroad.

5.5 Malaria

5.5.1 General considerations

Malaria is a common and serious tropical disease. It is a protozoal infection transmitted to human beings by mosquitos biting mostly between sunset and sunrise. Human malaria is caused by four species of *Plasmodium: Plasmodium falciparum, P. vivax, P. ovale,* and *P. malariae.* Travellers to malarious areas often run a high risk of acquiring the disease; each year many travellers fall ill with malaria while visiting countries where the disease is endemic, and more than 10 000 fall ill on return to their home countries. About 1% of people with *P. falciparum* infection die. Most of these deaths could be prevented by earlier diagnosis and adequate treatment.

The malaria situation is getting worse in many areas, and prevention and treatment of falciparum malaria are becoming more difficult because the resistance of the parasite to antimalarial drugs is increasing and becoming more widespread.

In many countries of Asia, the eastern Mediterranean area, and South America where there is malaria, the main urban areas are free of transmission of the disease, although this is not necessarily true of their outskirts or of main urban areas in Africa and India. While there is usually much less risk of malaria at altitudes greater than 1500 metres, the disease can occur in hot climatic conditions at altitudes up to 3000 metres. The risk of infection may also vary according to the season.

Health authorities are requested to draw the attention of travellers to the risk of contracting malaria in countries where it is endemic. Authorities in

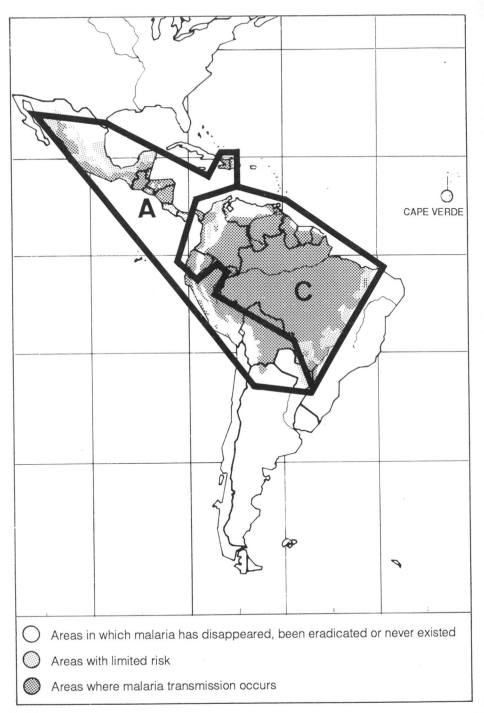

CAPE VERDE

A

C

○ Areas in which malaria has disappeared, been eradicated or never existed

◔ Areas with limited risk

◉ Areas where malaria transmission occurs

countries in endemic areas are required by World Health Assembly resolution WHA22.48 of 1969 to provide WHO regularly with information on the malaria situation in those countries. Although the data provided are not always complete, they are used by WHO to update the information given in this publication and to give an indication of areas of the world where malaria may be contracted and details concerning its prevention. A map (Map 3) showing the distribution of malaria in the world appears on pp. 68–69. Health administrations in travellers' home countries are encouraged to promote awareness among travellers of the risks and consequences of contracting malaria, of the limitations of antimalarial prophylaxis, and of the importance of measures to protect themselves against mosquito bites.

5.5.2 *Protective measures against malaria*

All travellers to malarious areas need to be well informed about the risk of malaria infection, and how they can best protect themselves (Box 5.1, p. 72).

All travellers should be told that protection from biting mosquitos is their first line of defence against malaria. Practical measures for protection are described in Box 5.2, p. 73.

The correct dosage regimen of the most appropriate antimalarial drug(s) (if any) for the place of visit should be prescribed (Map 3 and yellow pages). Prophylactic antimalarial regimens should be started one week before travel or, in the case of proguanil or doxycycline, the day before travel. Drugs should then be taken with unfailing regularity throughout the period spent in the area of malaria risk, and continued for 4 weeks after leaving the area. Drugs should be taken with food and swallowed with plenty of water.

No drug is devoid of side-effects, and the risk of serious, even life-threatening, adverse reactions dictates that prophylactic drugs should not be prescribed in the absence of a malaria risk. Not all travellers to countries where malaria exists should automatically be prescribed prophylaxis. This is especially true for tourists and business travellers who will visit only urban areas that are malaria-free. Some drugs are contraindicated in certain groups and individuals (see Table 2, p. 74, Box 5.3, p. 76, and Box 5.4, p. 78). Severe adverse reactions during prophylaxis with amodiaquine or sulfadoxine-pyrimethamine have led to their deletion from the list of drugs recommended by WHO for prophylaxis (Table 3, p. 77).

Both travellers and doctors should be aware that **no antimalarial prophylactic regimen gives complete protection.** Falciparum malaria, which can be fatal, must always be suspected if fever, with or without other symptoms, develops at any time between one week after the first possible exposure to malaria and two months (or even later in exceptional cases) after the last possible exposure. *The most important factors that determine the survival of patients with falciparum malaria are early diagnosis and appropriate treatment.* The symptoms of falciparum malaria may not be easy to recognize. It is important, therefore, that the possibility of malaria is considered in all cases of unexplained fever that starts after the seventh day of stay in an endemic area.

BOX 5.1
Checklist for prescribers

Travellers to areas of malaria risk should be:

1. Informed about the degree of risk of malaria infection (see country list in yellow pages and Map 3). Pregnant women and parents taking young children should question the necessity of their trip.

2. Informed how to protect themselves against mosquito bites (see Box 5.2).

3. Warned that they may contract malaria despite taking antimalarial prophylaxis.

4. Informed that malaria can kill if treatment is delayed. Medical help must be sought promptly if malaria is suspected and a blood sample should be taken and examined for malaria parasites on one or more occasions.

5. Questioned about drug allergies and other contraindications for drug use. If there is a known history of allergy, never prescribe similar drugs. If allergy is suspected, ask the patient to start prophylactic drugs early (e.g. 4 weeks before departure) and check the outcome before travel.

6. Informed how to take the prescribed antimalarial drug (*a*) for prophylaxis (drugs should always be taken with food and water) and/or (*b*) for stand-by treatment (see Map 3 and Tables 3 and 4).

7. Informed that prophylaxis must be continued for 4 weeks after leaving the malarious area, whether returning to their home country or moving to a malaria-free area in the tropics.

8. Informed that some antimalarial drugs can cause serious side-effects and that medical help should be sought promptly if these occur (see Table 2). If a serious side-effect occurs, the patient should stop taking prophylaxis. Mild nausea, occasional vomiting or loose stools should not prompt discontinuation of prophylaxis, but medical advice should be sought if symptoms persist.

9. Informed that symptoms of malaria may often be mild, and that malaria should be suspected if, one week after entry into an endemic area, they suffer unexplained fever with or without other symptoms such as headache, muscular aching and weakness, vomiting, diarrhoea, and cough. Prompt medical advice must be sought.

10. Reminded that they should only take stand-by treatment if prompt medical help is not available. They should complete the treatment course and resume antimalarial prophylaxis 7 days after the first treatment dose. Medical advice should still be sought after self-treatment.

11. Aware that if they have had, or have been suspected of having, malaria while staying in an endemic area, and have been treated or have used stand-by treatment, they should see a doctor for a check-up after returning home.

BOX 5.2
Protection against mosquito bites

The following measures are effective in reducing the risk of mosquito bites:

1. If possible, avoid going out between dusk and dawn when mosquitos commonly bite. Wear long-sleeved clothing and long trousers when going out at night, and avoid dark colours, which attract mosquitos.

2. Apply insect repellent to exposed skin, choosing one containing either N,N-diethyl-m-toluamide (deet) or dimethyl phthalate. The manufacturers' recommendations for use must not be exceeded, particularly with small children.

3. Stay in a well-constructed and well-maintained building in the most developed part of town.

4. Use screens over doors and windows; if no screens are available, windows and doors should be closed at night.

5. If accommodation allows entry of mosquitos, use a mosquito net over the bed, with edges tucked in under the mattress, and ensure that the net is not torn and that there are no mosquitos inside; increased protection may be obtained by impregnating the net with permethrin or deltamethrin.

6. Use anti-mosquito sprays or insecticide dispensers (mains or battery operated) that contain tablets impregnated with pyrethroids, or burn pyrethroid mosquito coils in bedrooms at night.

Before taking drugs for treatment, anyone suspecting malaria should promptly seek medical attention and insist that a blood sample is taken and examined microscopically for malaria parasites. If malaria is suspected but no facilities are available for blood examination, treatment should be started. If no parasites are found in the first blood film, but symptoms persist, a series of blood samples should be taken and examined at appropriate intervals.

P. ovale and *P. vivax* can remain quiescent in the liver for many months. Relapses caused by the persistent liver forms may appear months, and occasionally up to 4 years, after exposure. Relapses can be treated symptomatically with chloroquine and further relapses prevented by a course of primaquine, which destroys any remaining parasites in the liver. The normal adult dose of primaquine is 15 mg per day for 14 days, but in patients with known or suspected glucose-6-phosphate dehydrogenase (G6PD) deficiency (e.g. those of Mediterranean origin), expert medical advice should be sought since the drug may cause haemolysis in G6PD-deficient patients. Blood infection with *P. malariae* may be present for many years before giving rise to a symptomatic episode. The disease caused by this parasite is cured by standard doses of chloroquine.

Table 2. Special considerations in malaria prophylaxis and treatment[1]

Group	Recommendation
People with known or suspected allergies	• If history of allergy to sulfa drugs, antimalarials such as sulfadoxine–pyrimethamine and sulfalene–pyrimethamine should not be taken.
	• If history of allergy or other severe reaction to mefloquine, this drug should not be prescribed for prophylaxis.
	• If history of generalized psoriasis, chloroquine should not be prescribed. If history of severe pruritus after chloroquine treatment, use an alternative drug to chloroquine for prophylaxis.
	• Doxycycline may cause skin photosensitivity and should not be prescribed for people likely to be exposed to prolonged direct sunlight. Those who are sensitive should use a highly protective sunscreen and avoid prolonged direct sunlight or switch to another prophylactic drug.
People with chronic illnesses	• Seek individual medical advice (e.g. the normal doses of antimalarials may be toxic in those with hepatic impairment).
	• Mefloquine prophylaxis should not be prescribed for persons with a history of psychosis or convulsions.
	• Mefloquine should not be given to persons with known cardiac conduction defects.
	• Treatment with halofantrine is contraindicated in people with congenital Q–T prolongation.
People taking other drugs or vaccines	• Concomitant administration of mefloquine and other related compounds (e.g. quinine, quinidine and chloroquine) should be given only under close medical supervision because of possible additive cardiac toxicity. The prescribers should balance the risks and benefits of administration of mefloquine to travellers who are taking other drugs known to alter cardiac conduction.
	• Vaccinations with attenuated live bacterial vaccines, such as oral live typhoid vaccines, should be completed at least 3 days before the first prophylactic dose of mefloquine.
People who develop serious side-effects to an antimalarial	• Stop taking the drug and seek immediate medical attention; this applies in particular to neurological or psychological disturbances after mefloquine and to rashes after treatment with sulfa-derived antimalarials.

[1] Further information on adverse reactions, drug interactions, and additional contraindications is given in the manufacturer's prescribing information provided with the product.

Table 2 (continued)

Group	Recommendation
People who vomit	• Vomiting of antimalarials given for therapy is less likely if fever is first lowered with antipyretics and tepid sponging. A second full dose should be given to patients who vomit less than 30 minutes after receiving the drug. If vomiting occurs 60 minutes after a dose, an additional half-dose should be given.
People on mefloquine prophylaxis	• Treatment with halofantrine is contraindicated.
People involved in tasks requiring fine coordination and spatial discrimination (e.g. air crews)	• Mefloquine prophylaxis should not be given. After mefloquine treatment, caution should be exercised with regard to driving and operating machinery, and piloting aircraft should be avoided, since dizziness, disturbances of balance and neuropsychiatric reactions have been reported during and up to 3 weeks after the use of this drug. Chloroquine may cause blurring of vision and dizziness in some people; those affected should switch to another prophylactic drug.
People with a history of epilepsy or psychiatric disorder	• Mefloquine should not be taken (this includes people with a family history of epilepsy). Chloroquine should not be taken by people with a history of epilepsy.
Travellers needing emergency medication for presumptive self-treatment	• These people should use halofantrine only if known to have a normal Q–T interval.

5.5.3 Self-treatment

Most tourists and business travellers will be able to obtain prompt medical attention when malaria is suspected. However, a minority at risk of infection may be unable to seek such care within 24 hours of the onset of symptoms, particularly if they are in an isolated location far from competent medical services. In such cases, it is advised that prescribers issue antimalarial drugs to be carried by the traveller for self-administration ("standby therapy").

People prescribed standby medication should be given precise instructions on the recognition of symptoms, the treatment regimen to be taken, possible side-effects and the action to be taken in the event of drug failure. They should be made aware that self-treatment is a temporary measure, and that they should seek medical advice as soon as possible.

The choices of standby treatments in relation to the drugs used for prophylaxis are given in Table 4.

Halofantrine is no longer recommended for self-treatment following reports that it can result in prolongation of Q–T intervals and ventricular dysrhythmias in susceptible individuals. These changes may be accentuated if halofantrine is taken with other antimalarial drugs that can decrease myocardial conduction.

BOX 5.3

Advice to be given by prescribers to pregnant women and women of childbearing potential[a]

Pregnant women

1. Malaria in a pregnant woman increases the risk of maternal death, neonatal death, miscarriage, and stillbirth.

2. Do not go to a malarious area unless absolutely necessary.

3. Be extra diligent in the use of measures to protect against mosquito bites.

4. Take chloroquine and proguanil prophylaxis. In areas with chloroquine-resistant *P. falciparum*, chloroquine and proguanil should be taken during the first three months of pregnancy; mefloquine prophylaxis may be taken from the fourth month of pregnancy.

5. Do not take doxycycline prophylaxis.

6. Seek medical help immediately if malaria is suspected, and take emergency stand-by treatment (quinine is the drug of choice) only if no medical help is immediately available. Medical help *must* still be sought as soon as possible after stand-by treatment.

Non-pregnant women of childbearing potential

1. Mefloquine prophylaxis may be taken, but pregnancy should be avoided for three months after stopping the drug.

2. Doxycycline prophylaxis may be taken, but pregnancy must be avoided for about one week after stopping the drug.

3. If pregnancy occurs during antimalarial prophylaxis (except with chloroquine and proguanil), information about risks should be sought from the drug manufacturers by the woman's doctor.

---

[a] See also section 5.8.2, p. 85.

5.5.4 *Special groups*

Some groups of travellers are at special risk of serious consequences if they become infected with malaria. Foremost among these groups are pregnant women and young children.

Malaria in a pregnant woman increases the risk of maternal death, neonatal death, miscarriage, and stillbirth. Medical help should be sought immediately if malaria is suspected, and treatment with an effective antimalarial drug must always be given. Pregnant women should be advised not to travel to areas where transmission of chloroquine-resistant *P. falciparum* occurs. If travel cannot be avoided, great care must be taken to avoid mosquito bites (Box 5.2), and in the few areas where *P. falciparum* can be expected to be

Table 3. Drug regimens for prophylaxis and for treatment of malaria

(For recommendations according to the areas visited and to the age and other personal characteristics of travellers, see Table 2, Map 3, Boxes (Box 5.5 for paediatric doses) and text)

Drugs		Usual amount per tablet or capsule	Adult dose	
Generic name	Common trade names		For prophylaxis	For treatment[a]
chloroquine[b]	Aralen Avlochlor Nivaquine Resochin	100 or 150 mg (base)	300 mg (base) = 3 tablets of 100 mg or 2 tablets of 150 mg once a week, on the same day each week *or* 100 mg (base) = 1 tablet of 100 mg daily for six days per week	600 mg (base) on the first and second days, and 300 mg (base) on the third day (total 10 tablets of 150 mg or 15 of 100 mg)
proguanil[c]	Paludrine	100 mg	200 mg = 2 tablets once a day	not applicable
sulfadoxine-pyrimethamine	Fansidar	500 mg + 25 mg	not applicable	1500 mg + 75 mg = 3 tablets in one dose
sulfalene-pyrimethamine	Metakelfin	500 mg + 25 mg	not applicable	1500 mg + 75 mg = 3 tablets in one dose
mefloquine[d]	Lariam Mephaquin	250 mg	250 mg = 1 tablet once a week, on the same day each week	1000 mg (4 tablets) or 15 mg/kg of body weight, whichever is lower, in one dose *or* 1000 mg (4 tablets) initially, followed by 500 mg (2 tablets) 6-8 h later (see Box 5.5)
quinine		300 mg	not applicable	600 mg (2 tablets) 3 times a day for 7 days (total 42 tablets)
doxycycline[e]	Vibramycin	100 mg	100 mg = 1 capsule once a day	not applicable
halofantrine[b, f]	Halfan	250 mg	not applicable	500 mg (2 tablets) in one dose + 500 mg after 6 hours + 500 mg after 6 more hours (total 6 tablets in 12 hours)[g]

[a] This does not cover all aspects of treatment; it includes the regimens that can, under exceptional circumstances (see text), be used for self-treatment.

[b] Also available as suspension.

[c] Recommended only in association with chloroquine, see Map 3.

[d] The use of the higher treatment dose regimen is recommended for infections acquired in areas on the Thailand/Cambodia and Thailand/Myanmar borders only.

[e] There is relatively little experience with this drug, and knowledge of its efficacy and toxicity is limited.

[f] The manufacturer advises that this drug must not be administered with food. It is not recommended for self-treatment.

[g] The manufacturer advises that a second treatment course be taken one week later.

BOX 5.4

Advice to be given by prescribers to the parents of young children

1. Children are at special risk since they can rapidly become seriously ill with malaria.

2. Do not take babies or young children to a malarious area unless absolutely necessary.

3. Protect children against mosquito bites. Mosquito nets for cots and small beds are available. Keep babies under mosquito nets between dusk and dawn.

4. Give prophylaxis to breast-fed as well as to bottle-fed babies, since they are not protected by the mothers' prophylaxis.

5. Chloroquine and proguanil may be given safely to babies and young children. For administration, drugs may be crushed and mixed with jam.

6. Calculate the antimalarial dose as a fraction of the adult dose based on the age or weight of the child (see Box 5.5).

7. Do not give sulfadoxine–pyrimethamine or sulfalene–pyrimethamine to babies under 2 months of age.

8. Do not give doxycycline prophylaxis to children below 8 years of age.

9. Keep all antimalarial drugs out of the reach of children and store in childproof containers. Chloroquine is particularly toxic to children if the recommended dose is exceeded.

10. Seek medical help immediately if a child develops a febrile illness. The symptoms of malaria in children may not be typical and so malaria should *always* be suspected. In babies less than 3 months old, malaria should be suspected even in non-febrile illness.

100% sensitive to chloroquine, chloroquine alone may be used. In areas of chloroquine resistance, prophylaxis with chloroquine plus proguanil is recommended during the first three months of pregnancy. Clinical experience with mefloquine has not so far revealed any embryotoxic or teratogenic effect. Nevertheless, mefloquine should be used during the first trimester of pregnancy only if the expected benefit justifies the potential risk to the fetus. Women of childbearing potential should be advised to use contraception while taking mefloquine prophylaxis and for three months after stopping the drug (Box 5.3). Other drugs are either dangerous to the fetus or insufficiently investigated to be prescribed for prophylaxis during pregnancy. In non-pregnant women of childbearing potential, mefloquine or doxycycline can be given, but pregnancy should be avoided for three months after completing prophylaxis in the case of mefloquine, and for about one week in the case of doxycycline.

Children are at special risk since they can rapidly become seriously ill with malaria. Fever in a child returning from a malarious area should be considered to be due to malaria until proved otherwise. Every attempt must be

BOX 5.5

Approximate fractions of adult doses of antimalarial drugs for children

Sulfadoxine–pyrimethamine

Therapy:
(adult: total dose 1500 mg + 75 mg
= 3 tablets)

Age (yr)	Wt (kg)	Fraction
2–11 months[a]	<10	1/6
1–4	10–19	1/3
5–8	20–30	1/2
9–15	31–45	2/3
>15	>45	Adult

Sulfalene–pyrimethamine

Therapy:
(adult: total dose 1500 mg + 75 mg
= 3 tablets)

Age (yr)	Wt (kg)	Fraction
2–11 months[a]	<10	1/6
1–4	10–19	1/3
5–8	20–30	1/2
9–15	31–45	2/3
>15	>45	Adult

Chloroquine

Prophylactic dose 5 mg/kg
(adult: 300 mg base weekly)

Age (yr)	Wt (kg)	Fraction
<1	<10	1/8–1/4
1–4	10–19	1/4
5–8	20–30	1/2
9–15	31–45	3/4
>15	>45	Adult

Therapy:
over 3 days, 10 mg/kg, 10 mg/kg,
and 5 mg/kg
(adult: total dose 1500 mg base)

Age (yr)	Wt (kg)	Fraction
<1	<10	1/8–1/5
1–4	10–19	1/4
5–8	20–30	1/2
9–15	31–45	3/4
>15	>45	Adult

Proguanil

Prophylactic dose 3 mg/kg
(adult: 200 mg daily)

Age (yr)	Wt (kg)	Fraction
<1	<10	1/8
1–4	10–19	1/4
5–8	20–30	3/8
9–12	31–40	1/2
>12	>40	Adult

Mefloquine[b]

Prophylactic dose 5 mg/kg
(adult: 250 mg weekly)

Age (yr)	Wt (kg)	Fraction
<3 months	<5	NR
3–23 months	5–14	1/10–1/4
2–4	15–19	1/4
5–8	20–30	1/2
9–15	31–45	3/4
>15	>45	Adult

Therapy dose 15 mg/kg[c]
(adult: total dose 1000 mg)[d]

Age (yr)	Wt (kg)	Fraction
<3 months	<5	NR
3–23 months	5–14	1/12–1/4
2–4	15–19	1/4
5–8	20–30	1/2
9–15	31–45	3/4
>15	>45	Adult

Therapy dose 25 mg/kg[e]
(adult: total dose 1500 mg)

Age (yr)	Wt (kg)	Fraction
<3 months	<5	NR
3–23 months	5–14	1/12–1/4
2–4	15–19	1/3
5–8	20–29	1/3–1/2
9–15	30–45	1/2–2/3
>15	45–59	5/6
>15	>59	Adult

Halofantrine

Therapy: 3 doses of 8 mg/kg at 6 hourly intervals
(adult: total dose 1500 mg)[f]

Age (yr)	Wt (kg)	Fraction
<1	<10	NR
1	10–12	1/5
2–4	13–19	1/4
5–7	20–25	2/5
8–9	26–31	1/2
10–12	32–40	3/4
>12	>40	Adult

Quinine

Therapy: 10 mg/kg at 8 hourly intervals for 7 days
(adult: total dose 12 600 mg)

Age (yr)	Wt (kg)	Fraction
<2	<15	1/8
2–4	15–19	1/4
5–8	20–30	1/2
9–15	31–45	3/4
>15	>45	Adult

Doxycycline

Prophylactic dose 1.5 mg/kg
(adult: 100 mg daily)

Age (yr)	Wt (kg)	Fraction
<1–7	<30	CI
8–12	31–40	NA
>12	>40	Adult

CI = contraindicated.

NR = not recommended because of insufficient data. However, if nothing else is available, may be administered in an emergency.

NA = not applicable. It is not practical to give fractions of adult dose (capsules) to children under 12 years of age.

[a] Not recommended below 2 months of age.

[b] Experience with mefloquine in infants under 3 months old or weighing less than 5 kg is limited.

[c] For all endemic areas except those on the Thailand/Cambodia and Thailand/Myanmar borders.

[d] Data on non-immune subjects weighing more than 60 kg are insufficient to conclude that this regimen will result in radical cure in all cases. Close medical follow-up must therefore be assured after treatment.

[e] For border areas of Thailand with Cambodia and Myanmar; to be given as an initial dose of 15 mg/kg followed 6-8 h later by 10 mg/kg.

[f] The manufacturer recommends that a second full course is taken one week after completing the first course.

made to seek prompt medical help, even if stand-by treatment is given. It is advisable not to take babies and young children to malarious areas, in particular to endemic areas where there is transmission of chloroquine-resistant *P. falciparum*. If unavoidable, they should be well protected against mosquito bites and receive malaria prophylaxis (Box 5.4). It may sometimes be difficult to administer an adequate prophylactic dose of a drug because of the small amounts required and the absence of paediatric formulations (see Box 5.5 for fractions of adult doses).

BOX 5.6

Advice to be given by prescribers to those intending to stay in a malarious area for over one month

1. Self-protection against mosquito bites must be maintained.

2. Continue to take the antimalarial prophylaxis recommended unless local doctors with experience in malaria suggest a more effective (and safe) alternative (e.g. tailor antimalarial prophylaxis to transmission seasons). Dosages of prophylactic drugs should not be reduced.

3. "Be prepared" for an attack of malaria. Know the symptoms of the disease and identify in advance local doctors experienced in treating malaria. If this cannot be done (e.g. during overland travel), adequate doses of stand-by antimalarials for emergency self-treatment should be carried (e.g. three treatment courses for 6 months of travel).

4. Always have an emergency treatment course of antimalarials for stand-by treatment in case prompt medical help is unavailable.

5. Twice-yearly screening for the detection of early retinal changes should be performed in anyone who has taken 300 mg of chloroquine weekly for over five years (screen after three years if daily doses of 100 mg have been taken).

The recommendations given throughout this section are applicable only to non-immune travellers visiting malarious areas for up to one month, which includes most travellers. It is difficult to give general recommendations for safe and effective prophylaxis for people who stay in malarious areas for longer than one month. The risk of serious side-effects associated with taking prophylactic chloroquine and proguanil is low. Data indicate no increased risk of serious side-effects with long-term use of mefloquine. The risk of serious side-effects from prolonged use of doxycycline is not yet known. Mefloquine and doxycycline should be reserved for those at greatest risk of infection (see Map 3). Those who stay in malarious areas for many months should be advised that they may suffer attacks of the disease (Box 5.6) and informed about how to deal with them. People intending to settle in malarious areas should be encouraged to identify local doctors experienced in treating malaria.

5.5.5 *Special situations — multidrug-resistant malaria*

In areas of Thailand near the borders with Cambodia and Myanmar, *P. falciparum* infections do not respond to treatment with chloroquine or sulfadoxine–pyrimethamine, and sensitivity to quinine is reduced. Treatment failures of over 50% with mefloquine are also being reported. A similar situation is reported from western Cambodia.

In these situations, chemoprophylaxis with doxycycline is recommended along with rigorous use of personal protection measures. Doxycycline should

Table 4. Choice of standby treatment according to chemoprophylactic regimen

Prophylactic regimen	Standby treatment
none	chloroquine (zone A; see Map 3)
none	• sulfa/pyrimethamine combination (zone B (see Map 3) and Africa south of the Sahara only)
	• mefloquine, 15 mg/kg
	• quinine
chloroquine alone or with proguanil	• sulfa/pyrimethamine combination (zone B (see Map 3) and Africa south of the Sahara only)
	• mefloquine, 15 mg/kg
	• quinine
mefloquine	• sulfa/pyrimethamine combination (Africa south of the Sahara only)
	• quinine
	• quinine + tetracycline, for 7 days
doxycycline	• mefloquine, 25 mg/kg
	• quinine + tetracycline, for 7 days

be taken daily, according to the schedule given in Table 3 and Box 5.5, with copious volumes of water to prevent possible oesophageal irritation. Light-skinned people may need to protect themselves from sunlight since the drug may induce photosensitivity. Experience with use of this drug for long-term chemoprophylaxis, i.e. over 4–6 months, is limited.

Doxycycline is contraindicated in pregnant women and children under the age of 8 years. There is no prophylactic regimen that is both effective and safe for these groups. It is advised, therefore, that expatriate women who are pregnant or who wish to become pregnant, and young children, should avoid entering these malarious areas.

Anyone experiencing adverse reactions to doxycycline chemoprophylaxis or with suspected malaria should promptly seek medical attention. Infections with *P. falciparum* acquired on the Thailand/Cambodia and Thailand/Myanmar borders may be cured with a total dose of 25 mg/kg mefloquine, given as 15 mg/kg initially followed 6–8 h later by 10 mg/kg, or with oral quinine, 10 mg/kg of body weight every 8 hours for 7 days, plus oral tetracycline, 500 mg every 8 hours for 7 days, if full compliance is obtained.

5.6 Dengue and dengue haemorrhagic fever

Dengue, and its complications, dengue haemorrhagic fever (DHF) and dengue shock syndrome (DSS), are the most important arbovirus diseases in the world today.

Dengue viruses are transmitted to humans by mosquitos, especially *Aedes aegypti*, a species that is well adapted to life in tropical urban environments. Unlike most malaria vectors, this species preferentially feeds on humans during the day, frequently enters homes to rest and feed, and breeds in water that is stored or collects around human dwellings. As a result, *A. aegypti* has invaded urban, suburban and rural settings throughout many parts of the tropics. Consequently, travellers to tropical countries, especially in southeast Asia and Latin America, may be at risk of dengue infection. At present, there is no protective vaccine for dengue, so travellers must rely on preventing mosquito bites to combat infection. In addition to taking the precautions suggested in Box 5.2, p. 73, travellers should use insect repellents or mosquito coils during daylight hours.

Anyone suspected of being infected with dengue, especially with haemorrhagic manifestations, should seek medical assistance immediately. If untreated or inappropriately treated, DHF and DSS have a high case-fatality rate; appropriate clinical management can reduce the rate to under 5%.

5.7 Vaccinations

Travellers can be immunized against a certain number of diseases. The duration of the protection conferred by immunization varies. It is possible to determine the person's immune status beforehand, but if there is any doubt it is usually more convenient to give complete primary vaccination or a booster, as appropriate.

A distinction should be made between vaccinations *required* by countries by law for entry to their territory, vaccinations *recommended* by WHO for general protection against certain diseases, and other vaccinations which may be *advisable* in certain circumstances (Table 5). A vaccination plan should be established, taking into account the traveller's destination, overall state of health and current immune status, the duration and type of travel, and the time available.

5.8 Special situations

5.8.1 *Extended travel*

The recommendations given for short trips are usually valid but not always adequate for extended travel. Each case should be examined individually. Special vaccinations (Table 5) may be needed in some circumstances.

Table 5. Comprehensive list of vaccinations

Type	Primary series	Interval between doses	Lower age limit	Effective after:	Booster interval	Remarks
Required vaccinations						
Yellow fever	1 (live attenuated)	—	6 months	10 days	10 years	Validity of the international certificate of vaccination begins 10 days after vaccination (see section 2.4)
Recommended vaccinations						
Diphtheria, pertussis and tetanus	Infants: 3 (DPT, killed vaccine)	minimum 4 weeks	6 weeks	3rd dose	At 15-24 months of age	In some countries additional booster dose is given at or before school entry (4-6 years).
	Children: 2 (DT, killed vaccine)	minimum 4 weeks	6 weeks	2nd dose	6-12 months after the second dose	Given to children with contraindication to pertussis vaccine. Upper age limit usually 6 years.
	Older children, adults: 2 (Td* or TT**, killed vaccines)	minimum 4 weeks	Usually 6 years	2nd dose	6-12 months after the second dose	Additional booster doses every 10 years. Indicated for persons travelling to epidemic areas.
Poliomyelitis	Infants and children: 3 (OPV, oral live vaccine) *or*	minimum 4 weeks	None	3rd dose	At 15-24 months of age	Usually given simultaneously with DPT. In endemic countries, an additional dose is given at birth or at 9 months. Some countries also give booster doses before or at school age. Infants travelling should receive 4 doses of OPV prior to departure.
	3 (IPV, injectable killed vaccine)	minimum 4 weeks	6 weeks	3rd dose	At 15-24 months of age	Usually given as a combined vaccine with DPT. In some countries booster doses are given before or at school age.
	Adults: 2 (IPV)	minimum 4 weeks	—	2nd dose	6-12 months after the second dose	Indicated for persons travelling to epidemic areas. An OPV booster dose may be desirable for adults primarily immunized with IPV.
Typhoid	3-4 (oral live attenuated)	2 days	3 years	Last dose	1 year	Recommended for people travelling in conditions of doubtful hygiene (see page 62).
	1 (injectable Vi vaccine)	—	5 years	10 days	None	
Measles	1 (live vaccine)	—	9 months	10 days	In some countries second dose is given at 6-12 years	Available also as combined measles/mumps/rubella (MMR) vaccine.
Hepatitis A	1 (immuno-globulin)	—	1 year	Immediately	3-6 months	Preventive immunoglobulin therapy is effective though of limited duration and hepatitis A vaccine is preferred when available. Indicated for travel to developing countries (see section 5.3.3).
	3 (injectable killed vaccine)	4 weeks	None	1st dose?	10 years?	
Hepatitis B	3 (killed, plasma derived or recombinant vaccine)	minimum 4 weeks	None	2nd dose	None	May be given at birth. Indicated for health professions and for people undertaking extended or frequent travel to countries of high endemicity (see section 5.4.2).
Other vaccinations						
BCG	1 (live attenuated)	—	None	2 months	None	Recommended for children and young adults expected to make an extended stay in an area of high tuberculosis endemicity. Contra-indicated for people with symptomatic HIV infection.
Cholera	1 (injectable killed)	—	1 year	6 days	3-6 months	Not very effective. Does not prevent transmission by carrier (see section 2.3).
Meningococcal meningitis	1 (type A+C) 1 (quadri-valent)	—	2 years	15 days	3-5 years	Indicated for people travelling in hyperendemic areas in close contact with the local population. Does not prevent transmission by carrier. To ensure long-lasting immunity, a booster dose may be required in young children.

Table 5 *(continued)*

Type	Primary series	Interval between doses	Lower age limit	Valid after:	Booster interval	Remarks
Rubella	1 (live)	—	12 months	Approx. 4 weeks	None	Women who fail to seroconvert after initial injection need to be revaccinated. Available as combined measles/mumps/rubella (MMR) vaccine, to be given after 15 months of age.
Mumps	1 (live)	—	15 months	2-3 weeks	None	Only available as MMR vaccine (see above).
Influenza	Children: 2 (injectable killed)	4 weeks	6 months	1 week after dose 2	1 year	The risk of exposure to influenza during foreign travel varies. depending on season and destination. In the tropics, influenza can occur throughout the year; in the southern hemisphere, the season of greatest activity is April-September and in the northern hemisphere, November-February. Elderly people and those with high-risk medical conditions preparing to travel to areas where influenza may be active should review their influenza vaccination histories. If they were not vaccinated during the previous season, they should consider influenza vaccination before travel.
	Previously vaccinated children:1	—	6 months	1 week	1 year	
	Adults: 1 (injectable killed)	—	—	1 week	1 year	
Rabies (pre-exposure)	3 (injectable killed)	7 days for 2nd dose, 28 days for 3rd dose	12 months	3rd dose	First after 12 months, then every 2-3 years	Indicated for high-risk occupations and situations in endemic areas (see section 5.2.7). Serum should be checked for antibody level 1 month after 3rd dose. Additional booster dose(s) should be given in case of exposure to a rabid or suspect animal.
Japanese encephalitis	2-3 (killed)	7-14 days	3 years (children under 3 years should receive half a dose)	10-14 days	1-4 years	Indicated for extended stay in rural areas of endemic countries (see section 5.2.6). Information on vaccine supplies should be obtained from the national authorities responsible for the protection of travellers.

* Tetanus-diphtheria vaccine with reduced amount of diphtheria toxoid for use in older children and adults.
** Tetanus toxoid.

The duration of travel must be taken into account when malaria prophylaxis is prescribed. Transmission of the disease may follow a seasonal cycle and, in areas where it is not continuous, it may be possible for the traveller to do without prophylaxis for a period.

5.8.2 *Pregnancy*

Travel is not generally contraindicated during pregnancy, but there are some risks; in particular, travel to malarious areas should be avoided if at all possible. Air travel is not recommended in the last month of pregnancy and until the seventh day after delivery. For safety reasons, airlines restrict the acceptance for international flights of women who are over 36 weeks pregnant.

Administration of killed or inactivated vaccines, toxoids and polysaccharides is authorized during pregnancy. Live vaccines are generally contraindicated. The risks and benefits should nevertheless be examined in each individual case. Vaccination against yellow fever is permitted after the sixth month of pregnancy when justified epidemiologically. Oral immunization against poliomyelitis is not contraindicated.

The antimalarial drugs chloroquine, proguanil and quinine may be given to pregnant women. Sulfadoxine–pyrimethamine, sulfalene–pyrimethamine, mefloquine, doxycycline and halofantrine are contraindicated during pregnancy (see Box 5.3, p. 76).

5.8.3   *Children*

Children usually adapt better to time and climate changes than adults. However, their resistance to illness is lower. A child can be overcome by acute dehydration within a few hours.

Air travel can sometimes cause discomfort to infants, who become distressed by the changes in cabin pressure. They should be given a bottle to help overcome the problem. Air travel is not recommended for infants of less than seven days old or for premature babies.

For children with sensitive skins, prickly heat can be alleviated by the use of talcum powder, daily bathing and loose cotton clothing (see section 5.2.4).

Some vaccines can be administered in the first few days of life (BCG, oral poliomyelitis vaccine, hepatitis A and B). Other vaccines (diphtheria/pertussis/tetanus, diphtheria/tetanus, inactivated poliomyelitis vaccine) should not be given before 6 weeks of age. Children can receive yellow fever vaccine from 6 months of age. Below that age, it is all the more important to ensure protection against mosquitos (see Box 5.2, p. 73). Special attention must be given to all children who have not been immunized against measles at the appropriate time. Measles is still common in many countries and travel in densely populated areas may favour transmission. For infants travelling to countries where measles is endemic, a dose of measles vaccine may be given at 6 months of age. However, children who receive the first dose at 6, 7, or 8 months should receive a second dose at 9 months or as soon as possible thereafter.

Malaria prophylaxis is important for children. Chloroquine, proguanil and quinine may be safely given to infants (see Box 5.5, p. 79). The prevention of exposure is vitally important, especially as it is relatively easy to protect small children by using suitable mosquito nets.

5.8.4   *Chronic diseases and other health problems*

Neither chronic disease nor advanced age is an absolute contraindication for travel. People suffering from chronic diseases or taking immuno-suppressive medication should seek the advice of their doctor. Drugs and medicines should be kept at hand so as to avoid the risk of an accidental break in medication.

Hot climates can exacerbate diseases of the cardiovascular and digestive systems, but may alleviate rheumatic pain and chronic infections of the upper respiratory tract.

Contraindications for air travel include cardiac failure, recent myocardial infarction or stroke, angina pectoris or chest pain at rest, rhythm disorders (e.g. paroxysmal tachycardia, left ventricular heart block, atrial fibrillation), uncontrolled arterial hypertension of more than 200 mmHg (27 kPa) systolic pressure, severe anaemia, sickle-cell anaemia, acute mental disorders, epilepsy, pneumothorax, and any serious and acute contagious disease. Passengers with a pacemaker should be made aware of the possibility of induction currents on board (from radar and electronic devices) and should take appropriate precautions. Passengers with rheumatism, arthritis, varicose veins and swollen legs are likely to experience discomfort on long-haul flights.

It is particularly important that travellers with a chronic illness should obtain information on the medical facilities available in the country to be visited.

5.8.5 *The disabled*

A physical disability is not a contraindication for travel. The airlines have regulations on conditions of travel for handicapped or disabled people who need to be accompanied.

6. MISCELLANEOUS

6.1 Blood transfusion

The decision to transfuse blood or blood products must be based on a careful assessment indicating that transfusion is necessary to save life or prevent major morbidity. Blood transfusion should not be the first consideration during the management of patients with acute haemorrhage, because blood volume replacement is initially more urgent than red cell replacement. Accurate diagnosis, adequate oxygenation and volume replacement with plasma substitutes (crystalloids and colloids), and prompt and meticulous surgical care may obviate the need for blood transfusion.

Blood that has not been obtained from carefully selected donors or that has not been appropriately tested for infectious agents should not be transfused, other than in the most exceptional life-threatening situations.

6.2 Medical kit for travellers

It is always useful to carry a disinfectant and dressings that can be applied easily. For travel to certain areas, sun creams, mosquito repellents, antimalarial drugs and oral rehydration salts are also basic necessities. Travellers should consult a doctor as to whether they should take antibiotics or antidiarrhoeal preparations with them.

Travellers contemplating a protracted stay in a remote location should consult someone who is competent to advise them on the content of their medical kit. If it is likely to be necessary to administer a vaccination or other drug by injection, disposable syringes and needles for this purpose should be carried.

6.3 Medical examination after travel

A medical examination is unnecessary after a short trip with no problems, or if the traveller has only suffered a trivial ailment (traveller's diarrhoea, cold). Patients with chronic diseases should nevertheless consult their doctor for a check-up. Medical examination is essential if fever, diarrhoea, vomiting, jaundice, urinary disorders, or skin or genital infections occur in the weeks following return from travel.

A medical examination is advisable after a long stay abroad. Some diseases do not develop immediately but may appear some time later when the traveller has resumed normal activities: the commonest of these are malaria, amoebic dysentery, viral hepatitis, typhoid and paratyphoid fevers, sexually transmitted diseases, intestinal parasitoses (e.g., giardiasis), schistosomiasis (bilharziasis), filariasis, leishmaniasis, trachoma, trypanosomiasis, and typhus. Travellers who fall ill on their return must inform their doctor of their trip without fail. Medical practitioners must always bear in mind that their patients may have been travelling recently and may have contracted an unusual disease. This is especially true for malaria, which may strike months or even years after the traveller has left the endemic area. Special attention should be paid to tuberculosis.

6.4 Note for travel organizers

Travel free of health problems is in the interest of travel organizers and employers as well as travellers.

Travel agencies are encouraged to give their clients objective information on the hazards related to travel and their avoidance. Awareness of vaccination requirements usually prompts travellers to seek medical advice. When no vaccinations are required, travellers are all too often ill-informed of the risks to which they may be exposed (including malaria).

Airlines and shipping companies that carry travellers to countries where malaria is endemic should ensure that their passengers are informed of the presence of the disease.

Travel organizations should be able to provide information on the medical facilities available at travel destinations (distance to the nearest hospital, facilities for evacuation in case of accident or emergency). When the destination is remote from any health care centre, the travel organizer should be able to provide specific products such as vaccines and antirabies or antivenom sera.

During the past decade, outbreaks of legionnaires' disease have occurred in some groups of tourists staying at certain hotels. This disease can present as a respiratory illness and may be severe and even fatal. The vehicle of infection is usually water; air-conditioning systems and showers have been implicated. Measures such as chlorination of water supplies can prevent infection, against which travellers have no other means of protection.

Codes of practice and recommendations on the application of specific procedures for the monitoring and safety of food and water have been established by such bodies as the International Air Transport Association and the International Civil Aviation Organization. These recommendations are brought to the attention of airlines and international hotel groups. The Joint FAO/WHO Codex Alimentarius Commission has so far drawn up some 25 codes of hygienic practice and/or technology in respect of different food products.[1] Some countries maintain extensive food surveillance activities at the national level. Travel organizations should ascertain whether these codes and recommendations are followed in the countries with which they are concerned.

---

[1] These are available upon request from national Codex Contact Points or from the Chief, Joint FAO/WHO Food Standards Programme, Food and Agriculture Organization of the United Nations, Via delle Terme di Caracalla, I-00100 Rome, Italy.

ANNEX

SOME RELEVANT WHO PUBLICATIONS

International Health Regulations (1969): Third annotated edition. 1983. 79 pages, index.

Ports designated in application of the International Health Regulations. Situation as on 1 April 1992. 1992. 40 pages.

Yellow-fever vaccinating centres for international travel. Situation as on 1 January 1991. 1991. 88 pages.

International medical guide for ships, 2nd ed. 1988. 376 pages.

Guide to ship sanitation, by Vincent B. Lamoureux. 1967, reprinted 1987. 119 pages.

Guide to sanitation in tourist establishments, by J. A. Salvato, jr. 1976. 129 pages.

Guide to hygiene and sanitation in aviation, by J. Bailey. Second edition. 1977. 162 pages.

Environmental sanitation in European tourist areas. Report on a Working Group, Montpellier, 1978. 1980. 33 pages (EURO Reports and Studies, No. 18).

Basic sanitation technologies suitable for smaller European communities. Report on a WHO Working Group, Rennes, France, 1978. 1982. 25 pages (EURO Reports and Studies, No. 34).

Guide to simple sanitary measures for the control of enteric diseases, by S. Rajagopalan; with a section on food sanitation by M. A. Shiffman. 1974. 103 pages.

Guidelines for drinking-water quality, 2nd ed. Volume 1. Recommendations. 1993. x + 188 pages. Volumes 2 and 3 in preparation.

Guide to shellfish hygiene, by P. C. Wood. 1976. 80 pages (WHO Offset Publication, No. 31).

Paralytic shellfish poisoning, by B. W. Halstead in collaboration with E. J. Schantz. 1984. 60 pages (WHO Offset Publication, No. 79).

Control of foodborne trematode infections. Report of a WHO Study Group. WHO Technical Report Series, No. 849, 1995, viii + 157 pages.

Mass catering, by R. H. G. Charles. 1983. x + 70 pages (WHO Regional Publications, European Series, No. 15).

Health surveillance and management procedures for food-handling personnel. WHO Technical Report Series, No. 785, 1989, 47 pages.

Safe food for travellers (leaflet).

The management and prevention of diarrhoea. Practical guidelines. 3rd ed. 1993. v + 50 pages.

The rational use of drugs in the management of acute diarrhoea in children. 1990. 75 pages.

Guidelines for cholera control. 1993. vi + 61 pages.

Cholera: basic facts for travellers (leaflet).

Prevention and control of yellow fever in Africa. 1986. v + 94 pages.

Vector resistance to pesticides. Fifteenth report of the WHO Expert Committee on Vector Biology and Control. WHO Technical Report Series, No. 818, 1992, v + 62 pages.

A global strategy for malaria control. 1993. x + 30 pages.

Implementation of the global malaria control strategy. Report of a WHO Study Group. WHO Technical Report Series, No. 839, 1993, v + 57 pages.

Management of severe and complicated malaria. Practical guidelines. 1991. vi + 56 pages.

Practical chemotherapy of malaria. Report of a WHO Scientific Group. WHO Technical Report Series, No. 805, 1990, 141 pages.

Malaria chemoprophylaxis. Reprinted from *Weekly epidemiological record,* 1985, No. 24.

Malaria chemoprophylaxis. Reprinted from *Weekly epidemiological record,* 1986, No. 15.

Malaria chemoprophylaxis regimens for travellers. Reprinted from *Weekly epidemiological record*, 1993, No. 51.

Drug alert: halofantrine. Change in recommendations for use. *Weekly epidemiological record*, 1993, 37: 269–270.

Development of recommendations for the protection of short-stay travellers to malaria endemic areas: Memorandum from two WHO Meetings. Reprinted from *Bulletin of the World Health Organization,* **66**(2): 177–196 (1988).

Epidemiology, prevention and control of legionellosis: Memorandum from a WHO Meeting. *Bulletin of the World Health Organization,* **68**(2): 155–164 (1990).

Dengue haemorrhagic fever: diagnosis, treatment and control. 1986. viii + 58 pages.

WHO Expert Committee on Rabies. Eighth report. WHO Technical Report Series, No. 824, 1992, 90 pages.

Management of patients with sexually transmitted diseases. Report of a WHO Study Group. WHO Technical Report Series, No. 810, 1991, 110 pages.

Sixth report of the WHO Expert Committee on Venereal Diseases and Treponematoses. WHO Technical Report Series, No. 736, 1986, 141 pages.

Control of sexually transmitted diseases. 1985. 110 pages.

Prevention of sexual transmission of human immunodeficiency virus. WHO AIDS Series, No. 6, 1990.

Guidelines on sterilization and disinfection methods effective against human immunodeficiency virus (HIV), 2nd ed. WHO AIDS Series, No. 2, 1989, iv + 11 pages.

AIDS in Africa. A manual for physicians, by P. Piot et al. 1992, 133 pages.

AIDS: images of the epidemic. 1994, x + 142 pages.

Control of Chagas disease. Report of a WHO Expert Committee. WHO Technical Report Series, No. 811, 1991, 101 pages.

Control of the leishmaniases. Report of a WHO Expert Committee. WHO Technical Report Series, No. 793, 1990, 158 pages.

Epidemiology and control of African trypanosomiasis. Report of a WHO Expert Committee. WHO Technical Report Series, No. 739, 1986, 127 pages.

Lymphatic filariasis: the disease and its control. Fifth report of the WHO Expert Committee on Filariasis. WHO Technical Report Series, No. 821, 1992, 77 pages.

Third report of the WHO Expert Committee on Onchocerciasis. WHO Technical Report Series, No. 752, 1987, 167 pages.

Sixth report of the Joint FAO/WHO Expert Committee on Brucellosis. WHO Technical Report Series, No. 740, 1986, 132 pages.

Prevention and control of intestinal parasitic infections. Report of a WHO Expert Committee. WHO Technical Report Series, No. 749, 1987, 86 pages.

The control of schistosomiasis. Second report of the WHO Expert Committee. WHO Technical Report Series, No. 830, 1993, vii + 86 pages.

WHO model prescribing information: drugs used in parasitic diseases. 1990, 128 pages.

INDEXES

INDEX OF COUNTRIES AND TERRITORIES

SUBJECT INDEX